*Dancing in Cambodia,
At Large in Burma*

By the same author
THE CIRCLE OF REASON
THE SHADOW LINES
IN AN ANTIQUE LAND
THE CALCUTTA CHROMOSOME

Dancing in Cambodia, At Large in Burma

AMITAV GHOSH

RAVI DAYAL Publisher
Delhi

Published by
RAVI DAYAL Publisher
51 E Sujan Singh Park
New Delhi 110003

Distributed by
ORIENT LONGMAN LTD
Bangalore Bhubaneshwar Calcutta Chennai
Ernakulam Guwahati Hyderabad Lucknow
Mumbai New Delhi Patna

© AMITAV GHOSH 1998

ISBN 81 7530 017 5

Typeset by Rastrixi, New Delhi 110070
Printed at Pauls Press, New Delhi 110015

Acknowledgements

Chapter 1 of the book appeared in a shorter version in *Granta* 44, Summer 1993; Chapter 2 in *The Observer Magazine*, 16 January, 1994; and Chapter 3 in *The New Yorker*, 12 August, 1996. The illustrations by Rodin are reproduced with permission from the *Musée Rodin*, Paris.

Contents

Dancing in Cambodia   1

Stories in Stones   54

At Large in Burma   65

*Cambodian dancers: four sketches
by Auguste Rodin, between pages 36–7, 40–1*

1
Dancing in Cambodia

1

On 10 May 1906, at two in the afternoon, a French liner called the *Amiral-Kersaint* set sail from Saigon carrying a troupe of nearly a hundred classical dancers and musicians from the royal palace at Phnom Penh. They were to stage the first ever performance of Cambodian classical dance in Europe, at the Exposition Coloniale in Marseille.

Also travelling on the *Amiral-Kersaint* was the sixty-six year-old ruler of Cambodia, King Sisowath, along with his entourage of several dozen princes, courtiers and officials. The King, who had been crowned two years before, had often spoken of his desire to visit France, and for him the voyage was the fulfilment of a lifelong dream.

The *Amiral-Kersaint* docked in Marseille on the morning of 11 June. The port was packed with curious onlookers; the city's trams had been busy since seven, transporting people to the vast, covered quay where the King and his entourage were to be received. Two brigades of gendarmes and a detachment of mounted police were deployed to keep the crowd from bursting in.

This enthusiasm cannot by any means be attributed to an

overly prolonged deprivation from the unfamiliar. On the contrary: for more than a month now Marseille had played host to the 'Exposition Coloniale', an immense fairyland of an exhibition, centred on the theme of France's colonial possessions; there was little by way of exotic and opulent fantasy that the exhibition did not offer, from Tunisian palaces to timber-studded West African mosques and Indo-Chinese pavilions. Indeed, within the vast panorama of France's overseas holdings, Cambodia with its four million or so inhabitants was a bare speck, its ruler no more than a minor potentate. Yet, no pasha or prince or bey had aroused nearly as much enthusiasm as the King of Cambodia and the royal dancers of his court.

The crowd had its first, brief glimpse of the dancers when the *Amiral-Kersaint* loomed out of the fog shortly after nine and drew alongside the quay. A number of young women were spotted on the bridge and on the upper decks, flitting between port-holes and clutching each other in what appeared to be surprise and astonishment.

Within minutes a gangplank decorated with tricoloured buntings had been thrown up to the ship. Soon the King himself appeared on deck, a good-humoured, smiling man, dressed in a tailcoat, a jewel-encrusted felt hat and a dhoti-like Cambodian sampot made of black silk. The King seemed alert, even jaunty, to those privileged to observe him at close range: a man of medium height, he had large, expressive eyes and a heavy-lipped mouth, topped by a thin moustache.

Following close beside the King, watching his every expression, were three pages. One of them bore a gold cigarette case, another carried a golden lamp with a lighted wick, and the third was the ceremonial bearer of a gold spittoon in the shape of an open lotus. This profusion of gold did not fail to dazzle the assembled journalists. Enquiring later, they learned, from M. Gautret, the French government's representative at King Sisowath's court, that the King had brought three trunkloads of expensive gifts with him, 30,000 francs worth: virtually every official and dignitary who had the good fortune to cross the King's path was to receive one. Indeed, the King had even insisted on bringing along a gift for the ex-President: 'What's to stop me from offering him a gift?' he had demanded of M. Gautret one day, and since the latter had been unable to think of a good reason, the ex-President too had been assigned his little bauble.

King Sisowath was an instant favourite with the Marseilles crowd. The port resounded with claps and cheers while the King took his seat in a ceremonial landau. His cortege was greeted by cheering crowds all the way to the Préfecture, where he was to stay.

In the mean while, within minutes of the King's departure from the port, a section of the crowd had rushed up the gangplank of the *Amiral-Kersaint* to see the dancers at first hand. For weeks now the Marseille newspapers had been full of tantalizing snippets of information: it was said that the dancers entered the palace as children and spent their lives in seclusion ever afterwards; that their lives revolved entirely around the royal family; that several were the King's mistresses and had even borne him children; that some of them had never stepped out of the palace grounds until this trip to France. European travellers went to great lengths to procure invitations to see these fabulous recluses performing in the palace at Phnom Penh: now here they were, in Marseille, visiting Europe for the very first time.

The dancers were on the ship's first-class deck; they seemed to be everywhere, running about, hopping, skipping, playing excitedly, feet skimming across the polished wood. The whole deck was a blur of legs, girls' legs, women's legs, 'fine, elegant legs', for all the dancers were dressed in colourful sampots which ended shortly below the knee.

The onlookers were taken by surprise. They had expected perhaps a troop of heavily-veiled, voluptuous Salomés; they were not quite prepared for the lithe, athletic women they encountered on the *Amiral-Kersaint* : nor indeed, was the rest of Europe. An observer wrote later: 'With their hard and close-cropped hair, their figures like those of striplings, their thin, muscular legs like those of young boys, their arms and hands like those of little girls, they seem to belong to no definite sex. They have something of the child about them, something of the young warrior of antiquity and something of the woman.'

Sitting regally amongst the dancers, alternatively stern and indulgent, affectionate and severe, was the slight fine-boned figure of the King's eldest daughter, Princess Soumphady. Dressed in a gold-brown sampot and a tunic of mauve silk, this redoubtable woman had an electrifying effect on the Marseillais crowd. They drank in every aspect of her appearance, her betel-stained teeth, her chestful of medals, her close-cropped hair, her gold-embroidered shoes, her diamond brooches and her black silk stockings. Her manner was at once haughty and childlike, remarked one journalist, her gaze was direct and good-natured; she was amused by everything and nothing; she crossed her legs and clasped her shins just like a man: indeed, except for her dress she was very much like one man in particular — the romantic Duke of Reichstadt, *l'Aiglon*, Napoleon's tubercular son.

Suddenly to the crowd's delight, the Princess's composure dissolved. A group of local women appeared on deck, accompanied by a ten-year-old boy, and along with all the other dancers, the Princess rushed over and crowded around them, admiring their clothes and exclaiming over the little boy.

The journalists were quick to seize this opportunity. 'Do you like Frenchwomen?' they asked the Princess.

'Oh! Pretty, so pretty . . .' she replied.

'And their clothes, their hats?'

'Just as pretty as they are themselves.'

'Would Your Highness like to wear clothes like those?'

'No!' the Princess said after a moment's reflection. 'No! I am not used to them and perhaps would not know how to wear them. But they are still pretty . . . oh! Yes . . .'

And with that she sank into what seemed to be an attitude of sombre and melancholy longing.

2

In January 1993 I met a woman who had known both Princess Soumphady and King Sisowath. Her name was Chea Samy and she was said to be one of Cambodia's greatest dancers, a national treasure. She was also Pol Pot's sister-in-law.

She was first pointed out to me at the School of Fine Arts in Phnom Penh. It was January, only four months before countrywide elections were to be held under the auspices of the UN's Transitional Authority in Cambodia — known universally by its acronym, UNTAC. Phnom Penh had temporarily become one of the most cosmopolitan towns in the world, its streets a traffic nightmare, with UNTAC's white Land Cruisers cutting through shoals of careering scooters, mopeds and *cyclo-pousses*, like whales cruising through drifting plankton.

The School of Fine Arts was hidden from this multinational traffic by piles of uncleared refuse and a string of shacks and shanties. Its walled compound was oddly self-contained and its cavernous halls and half-finished classrooms were filled with the self-sustaining, honeycomb bustle of a huge television studio.

Chea Samy was sitting on a bench in the school's vast training hall; a small woman with the kind of poise that goes with the confidence of great beauty. She was dressed in an ankle-length skirt and her grey hair was cut short. She was presiding over a class of about forty boys and girls, watching them go through their exercises, her gentle, rounded face tense with concentration. Occasionally she would spring off the bench and bend back a dancer's arm, or push in a waist, working as a sculptor does, by touch, moulding their limbs like clay.

I had only recently arrived in Phnom Penh. I had become curious about King Sisowath and Princess Soumphady some months before, after learning of their journey to Europe in 1906. I had no idea whether Chea Samy had known Princess Soumphady or not; she seemed, if anything, too young, barely middle-aged, it seemed hardly possible that she would be old enough to know someone who was born in the last century. When I put the question to her at the end of the class her eyes widened. She repeated the name a couple of times, looking from me to the student who was interpreting for us as though she couldn't quite believe she had heard the name right. I reassured her: yes, I really did mean Princess Soumphady, Princess Sisowath Soumphady.

She smiled in the indulgent, misty way in which people recall a favourite aunt. Yes, of course she had known Princess Soumphady, she said. As a little girl, when she first went into the palace to learn dance, it was Princess Soumphady who had been in charge of the dancers: for a while the Princess had brought her up....

The second time I met Chea Samy was at her house. She lives a few miles from Pochentong airport, on Phnom Penh's rapidly-expanding frontier, in an area that is largely farmland, with a few houses strung along a dirt road. The friend who I had persuaded to come along with me to translate took an immediate dislike to the place. It was already late afternoon and she did not relish the thought of driving back through those roads in the dark.

My friend, Molyka, was a mid-level civil servant, a poised, attractive woman in her early thirties, painfully soft-spoken, in the Khmer way. She had spent a short while studying in Australia on a government scholarship, and she spoke English with a better feeling for nuance and idiom than any of the professional interpreters I had met. If I was to visit Chea Samy, I had decided, it would be with her. But Molyka proved hard to persuade, not because she grudged the time, but because she had lately become frightened of venturing out of the centre of the city.

Not long ago she had been out driving with a friend of hers, the wife of an UNTAC official, when her car was stopped at a busy roundabout by a couple of soldiers. They were wearing the uniform of the 'State of Cambodia', the political faction that then governed most of the country. 'I work for the government too,' she told them, 'in an important ministry.' They ignored her; they wanted money. She didn't have much, only a couple of thousand riels. They asked for cigarettes; she didn't have any. They told her to get out of the car and accompany them into a building. They were about to take her away when her friend interceded. They let her go eventually: they left UN people alone on the whole. But as she drove away they had shouted after her: 'We're going to be looking out for you: you won't always have an UNTAC in the car.'

Molyka was scared, and she had reason to be. The government's underpaid (often unpaid) soldiers and policemen were increasingly prone to banditry and bouts of inexplicable violence. Not long before, I had gone to visit a hospital in an area where there are frequent hostilities between State troops and the Khmer Rouge. I had expected that the patients in the casualty ward would be principally victims of mines and Khmer Rouge shell-fire. Instead I found a group of half a dozen women, some with children, lying on grimy mats, their faces and bodies pitted and torn with black shrapnel wounds. They had been travelling in a pick-up truck to sell vegetables at a nearby market when they were stopped by a couple of State soldiers. The soldiers asked for money; the women handed out some but they wanted more. The women had no more to give and told them so. The soldiers let the truck pass but stopped it again that evening, on its way back. They didn't ask for anything this time; they simply detonated a fragmentation mine.

A couple of weeks after that visit I was travelling in a taxi with four Cambodians along a dusty, pot-holed road in a sparsely inhabited region in the northwest of the country. I had dozed off in the front seat when I was woken by the rattle of gunfire. I looked up and saw a State soldier standing in the middle of the dirt road, directly ahead. He was in his teens, like most uniformed Cambodians; he was wearing round, wire-rimmed sunglasses and his pelvis was thrust out, MTV-style. But instead of a guitar he had an AK 47 in his hands and he was spraying the ground in front of us with bullets, creating a delicate tracery of dust.

The taxi jolted to a halt; the driver thrust an arm out of the window and waved his wallet. The soldier did not seem to notice; he was grinning and swaying, probably drunk. But when I sat up in the front seat, the barrel of his gun rose slowly until it was pointing directly at my forehead. Looking into the unblinking eye of that AK 47, inexplicably two slogans flashed through my mind; they were scrawled everywhere in Calcutta when I was the same age as that soldier. One was 'Power comes from the barrel of a gun' and the other, 'You can't make an omelette without breaking eggs'.

It turned out he only had the first in mind.

Molyka had heard stories like these, but living in Phnom Penh, working as a civil servant, she had been relatively sheltered until that day when her car was stopped. The incident frightened her in ways she couldn't quite articulate; it re-awakened a host of long-dormant fears. Molyka was only thirteen in 1975, when the Khmer Rouge took Phnom Penh. She was evacuated with her whole extended family, fourteen people in all, to a labour-camp in the province of Kompong Thom. A few months later she was separated from the others and sent to work in a fishing village on Cambodia's immense freshwater lake, the Tonlé Sap. For the next three years she worked as a servant and nursemaid for a family of fisherfolk.

She only saw her parents once in that time. She was sent to a market in the vicinity of Kompong Thom one day, with a group from the village, to sell fish. While sitting by the roadside, quite by chance, she happened to look up from her basket and saw her mother walking towards her. Her first instinct was to turn away; she thought it was a dream. Every detail matched those of her most frequently recurring dream: the parched countryside, the ragged palms, her mother coming out of the red dust of the road, walking straight towards her. . . .

She didn't see her mother again until 1979, when she came back to Phnom Penh after the Vietnamese invasion. She managed to locate her as well as two of her brothers after months of searching. Of the fourteen people who had walked out of her house three and a half years before, ten were dead, including her father, two brothers and a sister. Her mother had become an abject, terrified creature after her father was called away into the fields one night, never to return. One of her brothers was too young to work; the other had willed himself into a state of guilt-stricken paralysis after revealing their father's identity to the Khmer Rouge in a moment of inattention — he now held himself responsible for his death.

Their family was from the social group that was hardest hit by the revolution: the urban middle classes. City people by definition, they were herded into rural work-camps; the institutions and forms of knowledge that sustained them were abolished — the judicial system was dismantled, the practice of formal medicine was discontinued, schools and colleges were shut down, banks and credit were done away with; indeed the very institution of money, and even the exchange of goods and services, was banned. Cambodia's was not a civil war in the same sense as Somalia's or the former Yugoslavia's, fought over the fetishism of small differences: it was a war on history itself, an experiment in the re-invention of society. No regime in history had ever before made so systematic and sustained an attack on the middle class. Yet, if the experiment was proof of anything at all, it was ultimately of the indestructibility of the middle class, of its extraordinary tenacity and resilience; its capacity to preserve its forms of knowledge and expression through the most extreme kinds of adversity.

Molyka was only seventeen then but she was the one who had to cope because no one else in the family could. She took a job in the army and put herself and her brothers through school and college; later she acquired a house and a car; she adopted a child, and — like so many people in Phnom Penh — she took in and supported about half a dozen complete strangers. In one way or another she was responsible for supporting a dozen lives.

Yet now Molyka, who at the age of thirty-one had already lived through several lifetimes, was afraid of driving into the outskirts of the city. Over the last year the outlines of the life she had put together were beginning to look frayed. Paradoxically, at precisely the moment when the world had ordained peace and democracy for Cambodia, uncertainty had reached its peak within the country. Nobody knew what was going to happen after the UN-sponsored elections were held; who would come to power and what they would do once they did. Her colleagues had all become desperate to make some provision for the future — by buying, stealing, selling whatever was at hand. Those two soldiers who had stopped her car were no exception. Everyone she knew was a little like that now — ministers, bureaucrats, policemen; they were all people who saw themselves faced with yet another beginning.

Now Molyka was driving out to meet Pol Pot's brother and sister-in-law: relatives of a man whose name was indelibly associated with the deaths of her own father and nine other members of her family. She had gasped in disbelief when I first asked her to accompany me: to her, as to most people in Cambodia, the name 'Pol Pot' was an abstraction; it referred to a time, an epoch, an organization, a form of terror — it was almost impossible to associate it with a mere human being, one that had brothers, relatives, sisters-in-law. But she was curious too, and in the end, overcoming her fear of the neighbourhood, she drove me out in her own car, into the newly-colonized farmland near Pochentong airport.

The house, when we found it, proved to be a comfortable wooden structure, built in the traditional Khmer style, with its details picked out in bright blue. Like all such houses it was supported on stilts, and as we walked in, a figure detached itself from the shadows beneath the house and came towards us: a tall, vigorous-looking man, dressed in a sarong. He had a broad, pleasant face and short, spiky grey hair. The resemblance to Pol Pot was startling.

I glanced at Molyka: she bowed, joining her hands, as he welcomed us in, and they exchanged a few friendly words of greeting. His wife was waiting upstairs, he said, and led us up a wooden staircase to a large, airy room with a few photographs on the bare walls: portraits of relatives and ancestors, of the kind that hang in every Khmer house. Chea Samy was sitting on a couch at the far end of the room: she waved us in and her husband took his leave of us, smiling, hands folded.

'I wanted to attack him when I first saw him', Molyka told me later. 'But then I thought — it's not his fault. What has he ever done to me?'

3

Chea Samy was taken into the palace in Phnom Penh in 1925, as a child of six, to begin her training in classical dance. She was chosen after an audition in which thousands of children participated. Her parents were thrilled: dance was one of the few means by which a commoner could gain entry into the palace in those days, and to have a child accepted often meant preferment for the whole family.

King Sisowath was in his eighties when she went into the palace and his behaviour had become erratic in the extreme. He would wander nearly naked around the grounds of the palace, wearing nothing but a kramar, a bit of checkered cloth, knotted loosely around his waist. It was Princess Soumphady who was the central figure in the lives of the children of the dance troupe: she was a surrogate mother who tempered the rigours of their training with a good deal of kindly indulgence, making sure they were well fed and clothed.

On King Sisowath's death in 1927, his son Monivong succeeded to the throne and soon the regime in the palace underwent a change. The new king's favourite mistress was a talented dancer called Luk Khun Meak and she now gradually took over Princess Soumphady's role as 'the lady in charge of the women'. Luk Khun Meak made use of her influence to introduce several members of her family into the palace. Amongst them were some relatives from a small village in the province of Kompong Thom. One of them was to become Chea Samy's husband: the youngest, his brother, was a boy of six called Saloth Sar. He was later to become known across the world by his *nom de guerre*, Pol Pot.

Chea Samy made a respectful gesture at a picture on the wall behind her and I looked up to find myself transfixed by Luk Khun Meak's stern, frowning gaze. 'She was killed by Pol Pot', said Chea Samy, using the generic phrase with which Cambodians refer to the deaths of that time. The distinguished old dancer, mistress of King Monivong, died of starvation after the revolution: one of her daughters had been apprehended by the Khmer Rouge while trying to buy rice with a little bit of gold. Her breasts had been sliced off, and she had been left to bleed to death.

'What was Pol Pot like as a boy?' I asked, inevitably.

Chea Samy hesitated for a moment: it was easy to see that she had often been asked the question before and had thought about it at some length. 'He was a very good boy', she said at last, emphatically. 'In all the years he lived with me, he never gave me any trouble at all.'

Then, with a despairing gesture, she said: 'I have been married to his brother for fifty years now, and I can tell you that my husband is a good man, a kind man. He doesn't drink, doesn't smoke, has never made trouble between friends, never hit his nephews, never made difficulties for his children. . . .'

She gave up; her hands flipped over in a flutter of bewilderment and fell limp into her lap.

The young Saloth Sar's palace connection ensured places for him at some of the country's better-known schools. In 1949 he was awarded a scholarship to study electronics in Paris. When he returned to Cambodia, three years later, he began working in secret for the Indochina Communist Party. Neither Chea Samy nor her husband saw much of him and he told them very little of what he was doing. Then in 1963 he disappeared; they learnt later that he had fled into the jungle along with several well-known leftists and Communists. That was the last they heard of Saloth Sar.

In 1975 when the Khmer Rouge seized power Chea Samy and her husband were evacuated like everyone else. They were sent off to a village of 'old people', long-time Khmer Rouge sympathizers, and along with all the other 'new people', were made to work in the rice-fields. For the next couple of years there was a complete news blackout and they knew nothing of what had happened and who had come to power: it was a part of the Khmer Rouge's mechanics of terror to deprive the population of knowledge. They first began to hear the words 'Pol Pot' in 1978 when the regime tried to create a personality cult around its leader in an attempt to stave off imminent collapse.

Chea Samy was working in a communal kitchen at the time, cooking and washing dishes. Late that year some party workers stuck a poster on the walls of the kitchen: they said it was a picture of their leader, Pol Pot. She knew who it was the moment she set eyes on the picture.

That was how she discovered that the leader of the terrifying, inscrutable 'Organization', Angkar, that ruled over their lives, was none other than little Saloth Sar.

4

A few months later, in January 1979, the Vietnamese 'broke' Cambodia — as the Khmer phrase has it — and the regime collapsed. Shortly afterwards Chea Samy and her husband, like all the other evacuees began to drift out of the villages they had been imprisoned in. Carrying nothing but a few cupfuls of dry rice, barefoot, half-starved and dressed in rags, they began to find their way back towards the places they had once known, where they had once had friends and relatives.

Walking down the dusty country roads, encountering others like themselves, the bands of 'new people' slowly began to rediscover the exhilaration of speech. For more than three years now they had not been able to say a word to anyone with confidence, not even their own children. Many of them had re-invented their lives in order to protect themselves from the obsessive biographical curiosity of Angkar's cadres. Now, talking on the roads, they slowly began to shed their assumed personae; they began to mine their memories for information about the people they had met and heard of over the last few years, the names of the living and the dead.

It was the strangest of times.

The American Quaker, Eva Mysliwiec, arrived in the country a year after the fall of the Pol Pot régime, in 1980; she was one of the first foreign relief workers to come to Cambodia and is now a legend in Phnom Penh. Some of her most vivid memories of that period are of the volcanic outbursts of speech that erupted everywhere at unexpected moments. Friends and acquaintances would suddenly begin to describe what they had lived through and seen, what had happened to them and their families and how they had managed to survive. Often people would wake up in the morning looking worse than they had the night before: they would see things in their dreams; all those things they had tried to put out of their minds when they were happening because they would have gone mad if they'd stopped to think about them — a brother called away in the dark, an infant battered against a tree, children starving to death. When you saw them in the morning and asked what had happened at night, what the matter was, they would make a circular gesture, as though the past had been unfolding like a turning reel, and say, simply, 'Camera'.

Eventually, after weeks of wandering, Chea Samy and her husband reached the western outskirts of Phnom Penh. There, one day, entirely by accident, she ran into a former student of hers, who cried: 'Teacher! Where have you been? They've been looking for you everywhere.'

There was only the sketchiest of administrations in the country at the time. The Cambodians who had taken over the government with the help of the Vietnamese were all one-time members of the Communist Party of Cambodia; they had fled across the border when Pol Pot's clique launched its final, most bloodthirsty purges of the party. They had moved into a few ministries, but there was still nothing like a real government in Phnom Penh. The country was like a shattered slate: before you could think of drawing lines on it you had to find the pieces and fit them together.

The first priority now was the distribution of food; the second was to find those people with skills and knowledge who had somehow managed to survive the 'Pol Pot time'. The fledgeling Ministry of Culture had already launched an effort to locate the trained classical dancers and teachers who had survived. As part of its effort, the government made several radio broadcasts asking classical dancers to come to Phnom Penh. It soon found that dancers and musicians had been particularly hard-hit by the Revolution: by some estimates, as many as ninety per cent of the artistes of the pre-revolutionary era died during the 'Pol Pot time'.

The few who were still alive were in no state to start dancing again. 'I was like a smoker who gives up smoking', a well-known dancer said to me once, describing those years. 'I would dream of dance when I was alone or at night. You could get through the day because of the hard work. It was the nights that were really difficult; we would lie awake wondering who was going to be called out next. That was when I would dance, in my head.'

The officials of the Ministry of Culture were overjoyed to find Chea Samy. They quickly arranged for her to travel through the country to look for other teachers and for young people with talent and potential.

'It was very difficult', said Chea Samy. 'I did not know where to go; where to start. Most of the teachers had been killed or maimed, and the others were in no state to begin teaching again. Anyway there was no one to teach: so many of the children were orphans, half-starved. They had no idea of dance; they had never seen Khmer dance. It seemed impossible; there was no place to begin.'

Her voice was quiet and matter of fact but there was a quality of muted exhilaration in it too. I recognized that note at once for I had heard it before: in Molyka's voice, for example, when she spoke of the first years after the Pol Pot time, when slowly, patiently, she had picked through the rubble around her and built herself and her family a life of a kind. I was to hear it again and again in Cambodia — most often in the voices of women. They had lived through an experience very nearly unique in human history: they had found themselves adrift in the ruins of a society which had collapsed into a formless heap, its scaffolding systematically dismantled, picked apart with the tools of a murderously rational form of social science. They had had to start from the beginning, literally, like ragpickers, piecing their families, their roofs, their lives together from the little that was left.

Like everyone around her, Chea Samy too had started all over again — at the age of sixty, with her health shattered by the years of famine and hard labour. Working with quiet, dogged persistence, she and a handful of other dancers and musicians slowly brought together a ragged, half-starved bunch of orphans and castaways, and with the discipline of their long, rigorous years of training they began to resurrect the art that Princess Soumphady and Luk Khun Meak had passed on to them in that long-ago world, when King Sisowath reigned. Out of the ruins around them they began to create the means of denying Pol Pot his victory.

5

In Marseille, in the mean while, King Sisowath is in the process of being installed in his apartments at the Préfecture.

His Majesty King Sisowath the First had wedged himself into the throne of Cambodia some two years before; to be precise on 23 April 1904, a day before it fell vacant upon his half-brother Norodom's death. This alacrity was prompted as much by prudence as impatience. Sisowath had spent thirty-six years as Crown Prince, waiting to climb on, and besides King Norodom had left behind several sons who, in the opinion of many, had a better claim to the seat than did the Crown Prince, Sisowath. Fortunately for Sisowath, Cambodia's protectors, the French, did not share that opinion: Norodom and his sons had given them a great deal of trouble and they were only too glad to confirm Sisowath in the succession.

The relationship between Sisowath and Norodom had never been very good. King Norodom, who succeeded to his father's throne at the age of thirty, was fiercely protective of his sovereignty and bitterly resentful of the French. Limited though his powers were, he succeeded in thwarting and annoying the French for more than forty years. King Norodom's is, in fact, an immensely attractive as well as recognizable figure within the annals of colonialism: the doughty chieftain who defends his tiny corner of the world with courage and resourcefulness against overwhelming odds.

King Sisowath cuts an entirely different kind of figure: where Norodom matched his wits against the French, Sisowath, cooling his heels for thirty years in the pinched footwear of a Crown Prince, actively collaborated with them; where Norodom resisted every element of French cultural influence, Sisowath sent one of his sons to school in Marseille and made no secret of his wish to visit France.

Sisowath was not an imposing personage and his nephew, the icon of Cambodian nationalism, Prince Yukanthor, was probably right when he described him as a 'ridiculous figure who is an object of mirth for all Cambodians'. The role he chose for himself was not a romantic one, and nor has history been kind to him. But it may well be that one day he will be judged less harshly than he is now.

In any event, the months after King Norodom's death were in some ways the most important in Sisowath's reign. Within the first week, he reached an understanding with the French whereby he relinquished the last vestiges of power left to the king of Cambodia. He also handed over his palace to be used as the premises of a French-run school for Cambodians: this was to be in effect the first institution to make western education generally available to Cambodians. It was at this time also that the possibility of a trip to France was mooted, and King

Sisowath eagerly seized the opportunity to fulfil 'the dream of his whole life'.

France, for her part, went to great lengths to ensure the King's comfort. His apartments in Marseille for example, were selected and prepared with a great deal of thought, for King Sisowath was well known to be a man of unusual needs and habits. For one thing, he kept no fixed hours, generally rising very late in the morning and eating and sleeping whenever he chose. Besides, like his deceased brother Norodom (with whom he had shared a taste for wine and brandy as well as music and dance), it was his custom to pass his mornings by smoking opium with a few chosen members of his family and court. Having long kept the royal family supplied with premium-quality opium in Phnom Penh, the French could hardly do less in France. Thus appropriate arrangements had had to be made at the Préfecture, down to such details as providing the right kind of mat (*'Voila!'* cried the newspapers, 'An opium den in the Préfecture! There's no justice left!'). It was also the King's custom to dine alone, waited on by a few favoured women, secluded from his sons, daughters and ministers. The practice demanded a profusion of dining rooms, whereas the Presidential suite could offer but one: thus it was clear already that the etiquette of the Cambodian court was headed for injury in Marseille. Then there was the question of accommodating the women who had accompanied the King: it was true that he had brought only twenty favourites with him (a tiny number, as one newspaper pointed out, if one kept in mind the fact that there were over four hundred women in his palace in Phnom Penh). Still, for an apartment that had been designed with monogamous Presidents in mind, this was not an inconsiderable number to accommodate. Add to this a couple of dozen princes, princesses, ministers, pages and so on, and the

Dancing in Cambodia

number mounts into the reaches of a real administrative nightmare.

But in the event, all went well and the King and his entourage were successfully installed in the Préfecture. Shortly afterwards a group of reporters were allowed to visit the royal apartments to observe, as it were, the King and his court in what was to be their natural habitat for the next week. They found, to their satisfaction, that everything was *comme il faut*, to the point where a full-length portrait of the King had been positioned thoughtfully, in the dining room. Penetrating into the inner chambers they chanced upon scenes of domestic felicity tender enough to evoke raptures: 'They are absolutely at home there, and it is touching to observe the familial way in which they live, the respect with which the King is surrounded and the nobility of his conduct. We passed a half hour in this intimate atmosphere and brought away very pleasant memories'.

By now, to the despair of the gendarmerie, large crowds had gathered around the Préfecture in the hope of catching a glimpse of the King. They were to be disappointed however, for the King remained secluded in his apartment for the rest of the day.

Next morning he rose at the unaccustomedly early hour of seven and was immediately waited upon by six favoured women. After completing an extensive and meticulous toilette, he settled down with a few of his advisers to smoke a few pipes of opium and discuss matters of state.

It was not till four-thirty that the King, to the delight of the waiting crowd, appeared outside the Préfecture. The French public had long been warned that the King kept himself well-informed about modern France and that it was fruitless to expect him to be greatly surprised by anything he saw, or to expect him to provide any of those entertaining little instances of misrecognition and misunderstanding that so often enlivened encounters with foreigners. But it soon became clear that the authorities had been unduly pessimistic on this score.

That very evening for example, in front of a large crowd, the King came to a dead halt before an elevator at the Cathedral of Notre Dame de la Garde. Showing signs of evident alarm, he beckoned to his son, the handsome and debonair Prince Souphanouvong, who had been studying at a Lycée in Marseille for the last two years, and asked: 'Have you ever been on one of these?' It was only after being reassured by the Prince that he stepped in. But once he had attained the heights of the building he proclaimed himself delighted with the machine. As for the panoramic view of the city, the harbour, the sea, and the cupolas, minarets and pagodas of the Colonial Exhibition, the sight seemed to move the King, or so the journalists thought, to the very verge of tears.

These and other such incidents served to further endear the King to the Marseillais. Everywhere he went that day, large crowds gathered to catch a glimpse of him and every street he passed along resounded with enthusiastic cries of 'Viva Sisowath'. The King, for his part, was not above playing to the crowd, and on one occasion he delighted the assembled spectators by stopping the cortège to make two pretty young women the objects of his gallantry. Another time, when two women broke through to his cortège and handed over a superb bouquet (not omitting, of course, to include their cards with it) he made sure that they were each sent a gold ring, set with a diamond.

'That's gallantry for you, isn't it?' remarked one reporter. 'But won't there be a deluge of bouquets at the Préfecture now, and doesn't the King run the risk of running over a carpet of flowers every time he goes out?'

6

Everywhere he went on his tour of France, King Sisowath was accompanied by his Palace Minister, an official who bore the simple name of Thiounn (pronounced *Choun*). For all his Francophilia, King Sisowath spoke no French, and it was Minister Thiounn who served as his interpreter.

Minister Thiounn was widely acknowledged to be one of the most remarkable men in Cambodia: his career was without precedent in the aristocratic, rigidly hierarchical world of Cambodian officialdom. Starting as an interpreter for the French at the age of nineteen, he had overcome the twin disadvantages of modest birth and a mixed Khmer–Vietnamese ancestry to become the most powerful official at the court of Phnom Penh: the Minister, simultaneously, of Finance, Fine Arts and Palace Affairs.

This spectacular rise owed a great deal to the French, to whom he had been of considerable assistance in their decades-long struggle with Cambodia's ruling family. His role had earned him the bitter contempt of certain members of the royal family, and a prince even denounced the 'boy-interpreter' as a French collaborator. But with French dominance in Cambodia already assured, there was little that any Cambodian prince could do to check the growing influence of Minister Thiounn. Norodom Sihanouk, King Sisowath's great-grandson, spent several of his early years on the throne smarting under Minister Thiounn's tutelage: he was to describe him later as a 'veritable little king', 'as powerful as the French *Résidents-Supérieurs* of the period'.

The trip to France was to become something of a personal triumph for Minister Thiounn, earning him compliments from a number of French ministers and politicians. But it also served a more practical function, for travelling on the

Amiral-Kersaint, along with the dancers and the rest of the royal entourage was the Minister's son, Thiounn Hol. In the course of his stay in France the Minister succeeded in entering him as a student in the École Coloniale. He was the only Cambodian commoner to be accepted: the other three were all princes of the royal family.

Not unpredictably the Minister's son proved to be a far better student than the princelings and went on to become the first Cambodian to earn university qualifications in France. Later, the Minister's grandsons too, scions of what was by then the second most powerful family in Cambodia, were to make the same journey out to France.

One of those grandsons, Thiounn Mumm, earned considerable distinction as a student in Paris, acquiring a doctorate in applied science and becoming the first Cambodian to graduate from the exalted École Polytechnique. In the process he also became a central figure within the small circle of Cambodians in France: the story goes that he made a point of befriending every student and even went to the airport to receive newcomers.

Thiounn Mumm was, in other words, part mentor, part older brother, part bully and part leader: a figure immediately recognizable to anyone who has ever inhabited the turbulent limbo of the Asian or African student in Europe — that curious circumstance of social dislocation and emotional turmoil that for more than a century now has provided the site for some of the globe's most explosive political encounters. But Thiounn Mumm was no ordinary student leader: in Cambodian terms he was a member of a political dynasty, like the Nehrus or the Bhuttos.

Among Thiounn Mumm's many protégés was the young Pol Pot, then still Saloth Sar. It is generally believed that it was Thiounn Mumm who was responsible for his induction into the French Communist Party in 1952. Those Parisian loyalties were to prove unshakeable: Thiounn Mumm and two of his brothers have been members of Pol Pot's innermost clique ever since their days in Paris.

Few people in Cambodia think it particularly a matter of comment that Pol Pot and his ultra-radical clique share so many links with the palace. As a well-known political figure in Phnom Penh put it: 'Revolutions and *coups d'état* always start in the court-yards of the palace. It's the people within who realize that the King is ordinary, while everyone else takes him for a god.'

In this case, the proximity of the Thiounns and Pol Pot to the élitist, racially exclusive culture of the court may have had a formative influence on some aspects of their political vision: it may even have been responsible, as the historian Ben Kiernan has suggested, for the strain of 'national and racial grandiosity' in the ideology of their clique. That strain has eventually proved dominant: the Khmer Rouge's programme now consists largely of an undisguisedly racist nationalism, whose principal targets, for the time being, are Vietnam and Cambodia's own Vietnamese minority.

In 1992, a Khmer Rouge defector, describing the training he had received at political camps, told UN officials: 'As far as the Vietnamese are concerned, whenever we meet them we must kill them, whether they are militaries or civilians, because they are not ordinary civilians but soldiers disguised as civilians. We must kill them, whether they are men, women or children, there is no distinction, they are enemies. Children are not militaries but if they are born or grow up in Cambodia, when they will be adult, they will consider Cambodian land as theirs. So we make no distinction. As to women, they give birth to Vietnamese children.'

Shortly before the UN-sponsored elections of 1993, there

was a sudden enlargement in the racist vocabulary of the Khmer Rouge: 'white-skinned, point-nosed UNTAC soldiers' were added to the list of its enemies.

7

The more I learned of Pol Pot's journey to France, and of the other journeys that had preceded it, the more curious I became about his origins. One day, late in January, I decided to go looking for his ancestral village in the province of Kompong Thom.

Kompong Thom has great military importance, for it straddles the vital middle section of Cambodia, the strategic heart of the country. The town of Kompong Thom is very small: a string of houses that grows suddenly into a bullet-riddled marketplace, a mortar-blasted French-colonial school, a hospital, a few roads that extend all of a hundred yards, a bridge across the Sen river, a tall, freshly-painted Wat, a few outcrops of blue-signposted UNTAC-land and then, the countryside again, flat and dusty, clumps of palms leaning raggedly over the earth, fading into the horizon in a dull grey-green patina, like mould upon a copper tray.

Two of the country's most important roadways intersect to the north of the little town. One curves eastwards, towards Phnom Penh; the other leads directly to Thailand and the Khmer Rouge controls large chunks of territory on either side of it. For many years this was perhaps the most hotly-contested road in Cambodia, and the point where the two roads met was guarded by an old army encampment, controlled by the State. The perimeter of the encampment was heavily mined: partly to keep the Khmer Rouge out, but also to keep the State's own none-too-willing soldiers in.

Dancing in Cambodia

Here, in this strategic hub, this centre of centres, looking for Pol Pot's ancestral home, inevitably I came across someone from mine. He was a Bangladeshi sergeant, a large, friendly man with a bushy moustache: we had an ancestral district in common, in Bangladesh, and the unexpectedness of this discovery — at the edge of a Cambodian minefield — linked us immediately in a ridiculously intimate kind of bonhomie.

The sergeant and his colleagues were teaching a group of Cambodian soldiers professional de-mining techniques. They were themselves trained sappers and engineers, but as it happened none of them had ever seen or worked in a minefield that had been laid with intent to kill, so to speak. For their Cambodian charges on the other hand, mines were a commonplace hazard of everyday life, like snakes or spiders.

This irony was not lost on the Bangladeshi sergeant. 'They think nothing of laying mines', he said, in trenchant Bengali. 'They scatter them about like popped rice. Often they mine their own doorstep before going to bed, to keep thieves out. They mine their cars, their television sets, even their vegetable patches. They don't care who gets killed; life really has no value here.'

He shook his head in perplexity, looking at his young Cambodian charges: they were working in teams of two on the minefield — an expanse of scrub and grass that had been divided into narrow strips with tape. The teams were inching along their strips, one man scanning the ground ahead with a mine-detector, the other lying flat, armed with a probe and trowel, ready to dig for mines. By this slow, painstaking method, the team had cleared a couple of acres in a month's time. This was considered good progress and the sergeant had reason to be pleased with the job he and his unit had done.

In the course of their work, the sergeant and his colleagues had become friends with several Cambodian members of their team. But the better they got to know them the more hopeless seemed the country's situation. This despite the fact that Cambodians in general had a standard of living that would be considered enviable by most people in Bangladesh or India; despite the fact that Kompong Thom — for all that it had been on the battlefront for decades — was neater and better-ordered than any provincial town in the subcontinent; and despite the fact that the sergeant was himself from a country that had suffered the ravages of a bloody civil war in the early seventies.

'They're working hard here because they're getting paid in dollars', the sergeant said. 'For them it's all dollars, dollars, dollars. Sometimes, at the end of the day, we have to hand out a couple of dollars from our own pockets to get them to finish the day's work.'

He laughed: 'It's their own country, and we have to pay them to make it safe. What I wonder is: what will they do when we're gone?'

I told him what a long-time foreign resident of Phnom Penh had said to me: that Cambodia was a country that was actually only fifteen years old; that it had managed remarkably well considering it had been built up almost from scratch after the fall of the Pol Pot regime in 1979; and that this had been achieved in a situation of near-complete international isolation. Europe and Japan had received massive amounts of aid after the Second World War, but Cambodia, which had been subjected to one of the heaviest bombings in the history of war and had then had to live through a bloody and destructive revolution, got virtually nothing. Yet Cambodians had made do with what they had.

But the sergeant was looking for large-scale proofs of progress — roads, a functioning postal system, Projects, Schemes, Plans — and their lack rendered meaningless those tiny, cumulative efforts by which individuals and families reclaim their lives — a shutter repaired, a class taught, a palm-tree tended — which are no longer noticeable once they are done since they sink into the order of normalcy, where they belong, and cease to be acts of affirmation and hope. He was the smallest of cogs in the vast machinery of the UN, but, no less than the most powerful bureaucrats and experts in Phnom Penh, his vision of the country was organized around his part in saving it from itself.

'What Cambodians are good at is destruction', he said. 'They know nothing about building — about putting things up and carrying on.'

He waved good-naturedly at the Cambodians and they waved back, bobbing their heads, smiling and bowing. Both sides were working hard at their jobs, the expert and the amateur, the feckless and the responsible: the doughty rescuer and the hapless rescued were both taking their roles equally seriously.

8

Suddenly the sergeant's walkie-talkie began to crackle. One of his officers was calling from the nearby headquarters of an Indonesian battalion. A very senior officer, a General, had just flown in from Phnom Penh in a helicopter; he would soon be driving past the de-mining centre on his way to inspect another UN unit. The sergeant was to make sure that that morning's haul of mines was detonated at the precise moment when the motorcade went past the de-mining centre as a kind of salute. He was to try and make as big a bang as possible; the General would be pleased; it would make a good impression.

The sergeant quickly set everything up and the unit took its positions. Motorolas crackled furiously; everybody waited, sweating, expectant, but there was no sign of a motorcade. Finally, worried about missing the mid-day prayers at the mosque, the sergeant gave up.

The General missed his bangs. It turned out that the Indonesians had managed to keep him for lunch.

The sergeant thought I was mad to come to Kompong Thom enquiring about a long-dead dancer, even if she was Pol Pot's cousin. Dance makes nothing happen, he might have said, especially in places where shelling is a nightly ritual and children regularly have their legs blown off by mines.

Later I got a ride with an Austrian colonel, in an UNTAC car, a white, airconditioned Land Cruiser. He was a small, dapper, extremely loquacious man: he'd spent most of his working life on UN missions; he rated the Cambodia operation well above Lebanon, a little below Cyprus. But he was still planning to get out of Kompong Thom — too much tension, guns going off all the time.

We stopped to pick up a Russian colonel, a huge man, pear-shaped, like a belly dancer gone to seed. His khaki shorts looked like bikini briefs on his gigantic legs.

The Russian reached for the radio, which was tuned to the UNTAC radio station, and turned it off: 'Yap, yap, yap, yap', he said, glaring at the Austrian.

The Austrian shrank back, but plunged into battle a couple of minutes later, moustache bristling. 'I like that station', he cried. His voice was high, terrier-like. 'I like it, I want to listen to it.'

The Russian jammed a tree-stump of a knee across the radio and looked casually out of the window. The Austrian snatched his hand back, but his defeat was only temporary. He turned to look out of the window and sighed. 'Such a beautiful country,' he said, 'such wonderful people — always smiling. But why are they always at war? Why can't they get on with building their country?'

He grinned at the Russian: 'I suppose we'll be going to Russia next — eh, my friend?'

The Russian sprang bolt upright, sputtering. The veins on his temples bulged. 'No,' he barked, 'no, not Russia, never, maybe Ukraine . . . but not Russia, never.'

Then a truck appeared on the road ahead of us, gradually taking shape within a cloud of dust. It was packed with people, many of whom seemed to be wearing olive-green fatigues. A man was leaning over the driver's cabin, looking directly at us: he had an unusual-looking cap on his head. It was green and looked Chinese, like something a Khmer Rouge guerilla might wear. The Russian and the Austrian were suddenly on the edge of their seats, straining forward.

The truck went past in a flurry of dust, the people in it waved, and we got a good look at the cap. There was lettering on it; it said: 'Windy City Motel'.

9

I got blank stares when I asked where Pol Pot's village was. Pol Pot had villages on either side of Route 12, people said, dozens of them, nobody could get to them, they were in the forest, surrounded by minefields. I might as well have asked where the State of Cambodia was. Nor did it help to ask about 'Saloth Sar': nobody seemed ever to have heard of that name.

One of the people I asked, a young Cambodian called Sros, offered to help, although he was just as puzzled by the question as everybody else. He worked for a relief agency and had spent a lot of time in Kompong Thom. He had never heard anybody mention Pol Pot's village, and would have been sceptical if he had. But I persuaded him that Pol Pot was really called Saloth Sar, and had been born near the town: I'd forgotten the name of the village, but I had seen it mentioned in books, and knew it was close by.

He was intrigued. He borrowed a scooter and we drove down the main road in Kompong Thom, stopping passers-by and asking, respectfully: 'Bong, do you know where Pol Pot's village is?'

They looked at us in disbelief and hurried away: either they didn't know or they weren't saying. Then Sros stopped to ask a local district official, a bowed, earnest-looking man, with a twitch that ran all the way down the right side of his face. The moment I saw him, I was sure he would know, and he did. He lowered his voice and whispered quickly into Sros's ear: the village was called Sbauv, and to get to it we had to go past the hospital and follow the dirt road along the river Sen. He stopped to look over his shoulder and pointed down the road.

There was perhaps an hour of sunlight left and we could hear the occasional rattle of gunfire in the distance. But Sros was undeterred; the thought that we were near Pol Pot's birthplace had a galvanic effect on him. He was determined to get there as soon as possible.

Sros had spent almost his entire adult life behind barbed wire, one and a half miles of it, in a refugee camp on the Thai border. He had entered it at the age of thirteen, and had come to manhood circling around and around the perimeter, month after month, year after year, waiting to see who got out, who got a visa, who went mad, who got raped, who got shot by the Thai guards. He was twenty-five now, diminutive but wiry, very slight of build. He had converted to Christianity at the camp, and there was an earnestness behind his ready smile and easy-going manner that hinted at a deeply-felt piety.

Sros was too young to recall much of the 'Pol Pot time', but he remembered vividly his journey to the Thai border with his parents. They left in 1982, three years after the Vietnamese invasion, because things were so hard where they were and because they'd heard, from acquaintances and from Western radio broadcasts, that there were camps on the border where they would be looked after and fed.

Things hadn't turned out quite as they had imagined: they ended up in a camp run by one of the Cambodian political factions, which was a kind of living hell. But they bribed a 'guide' to get them across to a UN-run camp, Khao I Dang, where the conditions were better. Sros went to school and learnt English and after years of waiting, fruitlessly, for a visa to the West, he took the plunge and crossed over into Cambodia. That was a year ago. With his education and his knowledge of English he had found a job without difficulty, but he was still keeping his name on the rosters of the UN High Commission for Refugees.

'My father says to me, there will be peace in your lifetime and you will be happy', he told me. 'My grandfather used to tell my father the same thing, and now I say the same thing to my nephews and nieces. It's always the same.'

We left Kompong Thom behind almost before we knew it. A dirt road snaked away from the edge of the city, shaded by trees and clumps of bamboo. The road was an estuary of deep red dust: the wheels of the ox-carts that came rumbling towards us churned up crimson waves that billowed outwards and up into the sky. The dust hung above the road far into the distance, like spray above a rocky coastline, glowing red in the sunset.

Flanking the road on one side were shanties and small dwellings, the poorest I had yet seen in Cambodia: some of them no more than frames, stuck into the ground and covered with plaited palm leaves. Even the larger houses seemed little more than shanties on stilts. On the other side of the road the ground dropped away sharply to the river Sen: a shrunken stream now, in the dry season, flowing sluggishly along at the bottom of its steep-sided channel.

It was impossible to tell where one village ended and another began. We stopped to ask a couple of times, the last time at a stall where a woman was selling cigarettes and fruit. She pointed over her shoulder: one of Pol Pot's brothers lived in the house behind the stall, she said, and another in a palm-thatch shanty in the adjacent yard.

We drove into the yard, and looked up at the house: it was large compared to those around it, a typical wooden Khmer house, on stilts, with chickens roosting underneath and clothes drying between the pillars. It had clearly seen much better days and was badly in need of repairs.

The decaying house and the dilapidated, palm-thatched shanty in the yard took me by surprise. I recalled having read that Pol Pot's father was a well-to-do farmer, and I had expected something less humble. But Sros was even more surprised than me: in Cambodia it was taken for granted that the relatives of politicians always got rich, one way or another. We were both brought up short by the house and the shanty beside it; there was something new and unfamiliar here: it was a reminder that we were confronting a phenomenon that was completely at odds with our quotidian expectations.

Then an elderly woman with close-cropped white hair appeared on the veranda of the house. Sros said a few words to her and she immediately invited us up. Greeting us with folded hands, she asked us to seat ourselves on a mat while she went inside to find her husband. Like many Khmer dwellings, the house was sparsely furnished, the walls bare except for a few religious pictures and images of the Buddha.

The woman returned followed by a tall gaunt man, dressed in a faded sarong. He did not look as much like Saloth Sar as the brother I had met briefly in Phnom Penh, but the resemblance was still unmistakable.

His name was Loth Sieri, he said, seating himself beside us, and he was the second-oldest of the brothers. Saloth Sar had gone away to Phnom Penh while he was still quite young, and after that they had not seen very much of him. He had always loved books; he read all the time, especially in French. He had gone from school to college in Phnom Penh, and then finally, to Paris. He smiled ruefully. 'It was the knowledge he got in Paris that made him what he is', he said.

He had visited them a few times after returning to Cambodia but then he had disappeared and they had never seen him again: it was more than twenty years now since he, Loth Sieri, had set eyes on him. They had been treated no differently from anyone else during the 'Pol Pot time'; they had not had the remotest idea that 'Pol Pot' was their brother Sar, born in their house. They only found out afterwards.

Was Saloth Sar born in this very house? I asked. Yes, they said, in the room beside us, right next to the veranda.

When he came back from France, I asked, had he ever talked about his life in Paris? What he'd done, who his friends were, what the city was like?

At that moment, with cows lowing in the gathering darkness, the journey to Paris from that village on the Sen river seemed an extraordinary odyssey. I found myself very curious to know how he and his brothers had imagined Paris and their own brother in it. But no. The old man shook his head: Saloth Sar had never talked about France after he came back. Maybe he had shown them some pictures — Loth Sieri couldn't recall.

I remembered, from David Chandler's biography, that Pol Pot was very well read as a young man, and knew large tracts of Rimbaud and Verlaine by heart. But I was not surprised to discover that he had never allowed his family the privilege of imagining.

Then the sons of the house came bounding up the stairs, a big, strapping man in his twenties, dressed in jeans and a T-shirt. He was friendly, but puzzled by our interest in his 'uncle'. He had never met him, and no less than anyone else, was hard put to conceive of a relationship between the house he lived in, the 'Saloth Sar' he heard his father speak of, and the name 'Pol Pot' and all it stood for.

Just before getting up, I asked Loth Sieri if he remembered his relative, the dancer Luk Khun Meak, who had first introduced his family into the royal palace. He nodded and I asked, 'Did you ever see her dance?'

He smiled and shook his head: no, he had never seen any 'royal' dancing, except in pictures.

It was almost dark now; somewhere in the north, near the minefield, there was the sound of gunfire. We got up to go, and the whole family walked down with us. After I had said goodbye and was about to climb on to the scooter, Sros whispered in my ear that it might be a good idea to give the old man some money. I had not thought of it; I took some money out of my pocket and put it in his hands.

He made a gesture of acknowledgement, and as we were about to leave he said a few words to Sros.

'What did he say?' I asked Sros, when we were back on the road.

Shouting above the wind, Sros said: 'He asked me: "Do you think there will be peace now?"'

'And what did you tell him?' I asked.

'I told him, "I wish I could say yes."'

10

On 10 July 1906, one month after their arrival in France, the dancers performed at a reception given by the Minister of Colonies in the Bois du Boulogne in Paris. 'Never has there been a more brilliant Parisian fête,' said *Le Figaro*, 'nor one with such novel charm.' Invitations were furiously sought after, and on the night of the performance carriages and cars trooped through the park like an 'army of fireflies'.

While the performance was in progress a correspondent spotted the most celebrated Parisian of all in the audience, the bearded Mosaic figure of 'the great Rodin . . . [going] into ecstasies over the little virgins of Phnom Penh, whose immaterial silhouettes he drew with infinite love . . .'

Rodin, now at the age of sixty-six, France's acknowledged apostle of the arts, fell immediately captive: in Princess Soumphady's young charges he discovered the infancy of Europe. 'These Cambodians have shown us everything that antiquity could have contained', he wrote soon afterwards. 'It is impossible to think of anyone wearing human nature to such perfection; except them and the Greeks.'

Two days after the performance Rodin presented himself at the dancers' lodgings, at the Avenue Malakoff, with a sketchbook under his arm. The dancers were packing their belongings in preparation for their return to Marseille, but Rodin was admitted to the grounds of the mansion and given leave to do what he pleased. He executed several celebrated sketches that day, including a few of King Sisowath.

By the end of the day the artist was so smitten with the dancers that he accompanied them to the station, bought a ticket, and travelled to Marseille on the same train. He had packed neither clothes nor paper, and according to one account, upon arriving in Marseille and finding he was out of paper, he had to buy brown paper bags from a grocery store.

Over the next few days, sketching feverishly in the gardens of the villa where the dancers were now lodged, Rodin seemed to lose thirty years. The effort of persuasion involved in sketching his favourite models, three restless fourteen-year-olds called Sap, Soun and Yem, appeared to rejuvenate the artist. A French official saw him placing a sheet of white paper on his knee one morning; he 'said to the little Sap: "Put your foot on this", and then drew the outline of her foot with a pencil, saying "Tomorrow you'll have your shoes, but now pose a little more for me!" Sap, having tired of atomizer bottles and cardboard cats, had asked her "papa" for a pair of pumps. Every evening — ardent, happy, but exhausted — Rodin would return to his hotel with his hands full of sketches and collect his thoughts.'

Photographs from the time show Rodin seated on a garden bench, sketching under the watchful eye of the policemen who had been posted at the dancers' villa to ensure their safety. Rodin was oblivious: 'The friezes of Angkor were coming to life before my very eyes. I loved these Cambodian girls so much that I didn't know how to express my gratitude for the royal honour they had shown me in dancing and posing for me. I went to the Nouvelles Galeries to buy a basket of toys for them, and these divine children who dance for the gods hardly knew how to repay me for the happiness I had given them. They even talked about taking me with them.'

On their last day in France, hours before they boarded the ship that was to take them back to Cambodia, the dancers were taken to the celebrated photographer Baudouin. On the way, passing through a muddy alley, Princess Soumphady happened to step on a pat of cow-dung. Horrified she raised her arms to the heavens and flung herself, wailing, upon the dust, oblivious of her splendid costume. The rest of the troupe immediately followed suit: within moments the alley was full of prostrate Cambodian dancers, dressed in full performance regalia.

'What an emptiness they left for me!' wrote Rodin. 'When they left . . . I thought they had taken away the beauty of the world . . . I followed them to Marseille; I would have followed them as far as Cairo.'

His sentiments were exactly mirrored by King Sisowath. 'I am deeply saddened to be leaving France,' the King said, on the eve of his departure, 'in this beautiful country I shall leave behind a piece of my heart.'

11

The trip to France, 'the dream of his whole life', evidently cast King Sisowath's mind into the same kind of turmoil, the same tumult of shock and bewilderment that has provoked generations of displaced students — the Gandhis, the Senghors, and the Kenyattas, amongst thousands of their less illustrious countrymen — to close their doors upon the cold unfamiliarity of wintry Western cities and lock themselves into their rooms to pour their hearts out in letters, recording their impressions for those they had left at home.

Almost exactly two months after the King's departure from France, a document was issued from the palace at Phnom Penh, recording the King's thoughts on his voyage for the benefit of his subjects. The document began by exhorting the King's subjects to join him in thanking France and in expressing their 'imperishable gratitude towards her who is our Mother by adoption'. It continued: 'The visits that HM made to the great cities of France, his rapid examination of the institutions of that country, the organization of the different services that are to be found there, astonished him and led him to think of France as a paradise.'

The document was cast in the guise of a Royal Proclamation, but it was in fact a kind of essay in travel-writing. It explains the King's journey as a trip taken in order to 'study the institutions of France in their own setting, and the benefits that could result from putting them into use'. It was thus that the King had undertaken the dangerous and fatiguing voyage, and subjected himself to the pain of a long separation from his family and his people.

The essay begins with a preamble that could have been borrowed from any nineteenth-century ethnographic text: 'In enquiring into the initial causes of French law and customs, His Majesty was led to the following reflections, which he now communicates to his people for their careful consideration.'

The King's first set of reflections concerned, appropriately, the subject of government and, eccentric old man though he was, he seems to have seen through the silk glove of Western political rhetoric to the iron fist of its realities. The lessons in statecraft which he chose to cite appear to have been learned from Napoleon and Bismarck rather than Rousseau and Montaigne. Exhorting the officials of his kingdom to perform their duties properly, he observed that: 'None should hesitate to sacrifice his life when it is a matter of the divinity of the King or of the country. The obligation to serve the country should be accepted without a murmur by the inhabitants of the kingdom; it is glorious to defend one's country. Are Europeans not constrained by the same obligation, without distinction either of rank or of family?'

The King's greatest concern, however, was with what later came to be called 'development': with the improvement of his country's industry and agriculture. His hopes were invested

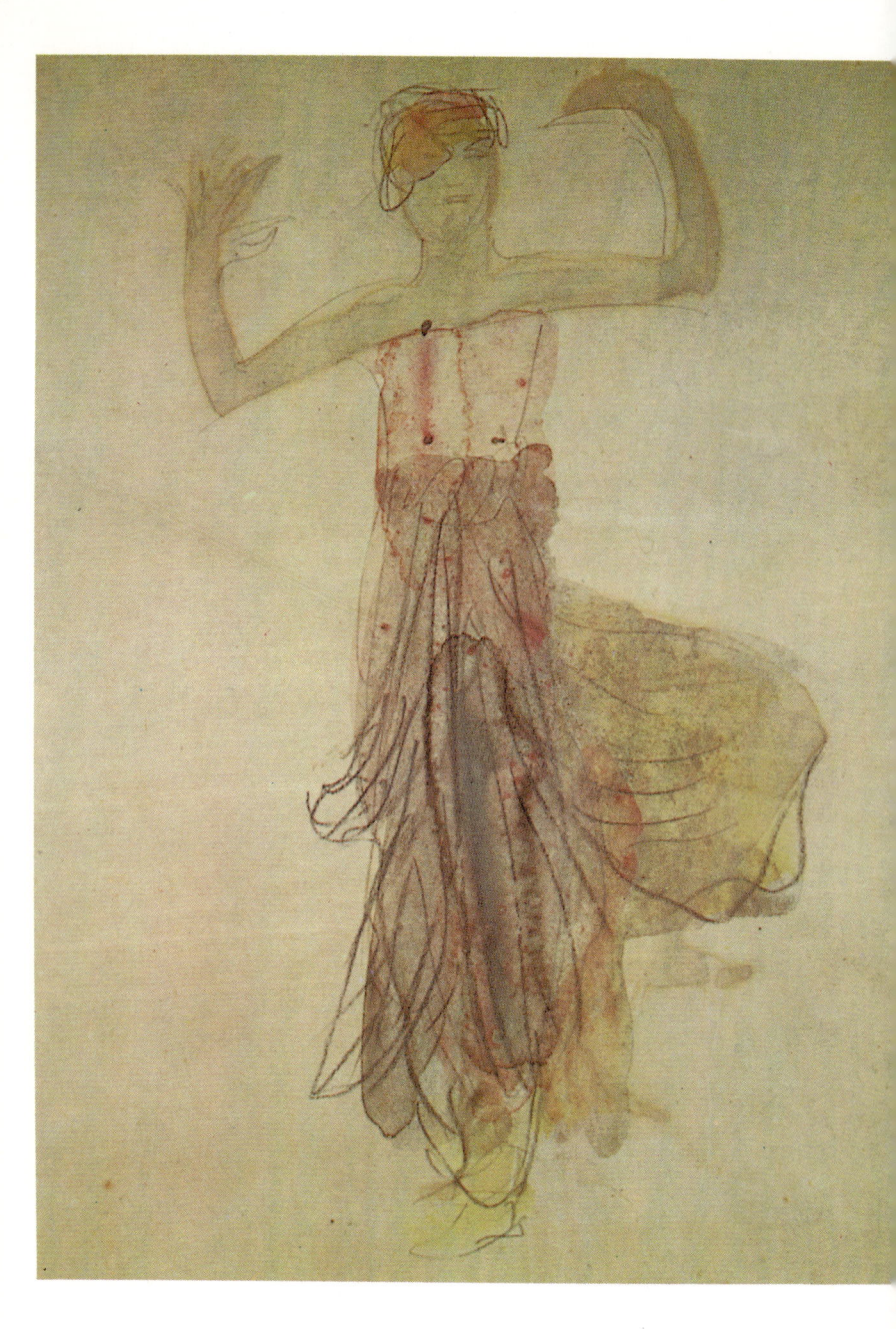

principally in improving his country's system of transportation: in France 'the cities are all linked to each other and the distances that separate them are crossed . . . within the space of a few hours. Before, it took entire days to cover the same distances'.

'In Paris,' continues the document, 'where there are almost three million inhabitants, the streets do not any longer suffice for the circulation of traffic; there is now an underground railway that directly links the different areas of the great capital to each other. Other savants are contriving to build balloons. The construction of these airships no longer present any difficulties; the only problem that has not been completely resolved is that of steering them. As soon as our network of routes is improved it will be possible . . . [for us] to have recourse to the same means of transport and to enjoy also the same advantages; there will no longer be long distances within our country.'

As for the rest, the King fell back on urgent exhortations, urging his subjects, in terms that eerily foreshadow the prescriptions devised by a later generation of Cambodian travellers to France, to start clearing new land for agriculture, to work harder in the fields, to raise more animals, to apply themselves to industry, to the exploitation of forests and fisheries, to familiarize themselves with modern machinery.

His own greatest concern in the future, he promised, would be to make his kingdom prosperous, to develop its intellectual resources and to increase the wealth of it people. In sum, the King had come to the conclusion, of which he now wished to inform his people, that: 'Emulation is the only means of turning resolutely to the path of progress.'

It is hard to imagine a more abject exhortation to mimicry: yet, this document is, if anything, a testament to the ambiguity of mimesis. For all the apparent servility of its tone, it makes no cultural or political concessions at all: the 'emulation' it calls for is entirely within the domain of technology and economics.

Thus, in a curious way King Sisowath's vision is the mirror-image of King Norodom's doughty nay-saying. And if his is the view that has come to prevail throughout South-east Asia, no one is likely to thank him for it.

12

Alas for poor King Sisowath, he was soon to learn that travel-writing was an expensive indulgence for those who fell on his side of the colonial divide. In 1910 the Colonial Ministry in Paris wrote asking the King to reimburse the French government for certain expenses incurred during his trip to France. As it happened, Cambodia's budget had paid for the entire trip, including the dancers' performance at the Bois du Boulogne. In addition, the King, who was ruinously generous by nature, had personally handed out tips and gifts worth several thousands of francs. In return he and his entourage had received a few presents from French officials. The French government now wanted to reclaim the price of those gifts.

For once, the obsequious Minister Thiounn took the King's side. He wrote back indignantly, refusing to pay for gifts that had been accepted in good faith.

The royal voyage to France found its most celebrated memorial in Rodin's sketches. The sketches were received with acclaim when they went on exhibition in 1907. After seeing them, the German poet Rilke wrote to the master to say 'For me, these sketches were amongst the most profound of revelations.'

The revelation Rilke had in mind was of 'the mystery of

Cambodian dance'. But it was probably the sculptor rather than the poet who sensed the real revelation of the encounter: of the power of Cambodia's involvement in the culture and politics of modernism, in all its promise and horror.

13

King Sisowath appears soon to have forgotten about his plans for his country's development. He was not, in any case, the kind of monarch who is destined to bend a nation to his will. Perhaps the most significant thing he ever did was to authorize the founding of a high school where Cambodians could be educated on the French pattern. Known initially as the Collège du Protectorat, the school was renamed the Lycée Sisowath some years after the King's death.

The Lycée Sisowath was to become the crucible for Cambodia's re-making. A large number of the students who were radicalized in Paris in the 1950s were graduates of the Lycée. Pol Pot himself was never a student there, but he was closely linked with it and several of his nearest associates were Sisowath alumni, including his first wife, Khieu Ponnary, and his brother-in-law and long-time deputy, Ieng Sary.

Amongst the most prominent members of that group was Khieu Samphan, one-time President of Pol Pot's Democratic Kampuchea and now the best known of the Khmer Rouge's spokesmen. Through the 1960s and early '70s Khieu Samphan was one of the pre-eminent political figures in Cambodia. He was renowned throughout the country as an incorruptible idealist: stories about his refusal to take bribes, even when begged by his impoverished mother, have passed into popular mythology. He was also an important economic thinker and theorist; his doctoral thesis on Cambodia's economy, written at the Sorbonne in the 1950s, is still highly regarded. He vanished in 1967 and through the next eight years he lived in the jungle, through the long years of the Khmer Rouge's grim struggle, first against Prince Sihanouk, then against the rightist regime of General Lon Nol, when American planes subjected the countryside to saturation-bombing.

Khieu Samphan surfaced again after the 1975 revolution, as President of Pol Pot's Democratic Kampuchea. When the regime was driven out of power by the Vietnamese invasion of 1979, he fled with the rest of the ruling group to a stronghold on the Thai border.

As the Khmer Rouge's chief public spokesman and emissary he played a prominent part in the UN-sponsored peace negotiations. Later, in the months before the elections, it was he who was the Khmer Rouge's mouthpiece as it reneged on the peace agreements and launched bloody attacks against migrant Vietnamese.

In 1991 and 1992, when Khieu Samphan was travelling around the world making headlines, there was perhaps only a single soul in Phnom Penh who followed his activities with an interest that was not wholly political: his forty-nine-year-old younger brother, Khieu Seng Kim.

I met Khieu Seng Kim one morning, standing by the entrance to the school of classical dance. A tall man, with a cast in one eye and untidy grizzled hair, he was immediately friendly, eager both to talk about his family and to speak French. Within minutes of our meeting we were sitting in his small apartment, on opposite sides of a desk, surrounded by neat piles of French textbooks and dog-eared copies of *Paris-Match*.

The brick wall behind Khieu Seng Kim was papered over with pictures of relatives and dead ancestors. The largest was a glossy magazine picture of his brother Khieu Samphan, taken soon after the signing of the peace accords, in 1991. In another picture the assembled leaders of all the major Cambodian factions feature: Prince Sihanouk, Son Sann of the centrist Khmer People's National Liberation Front, Hun Sen of the 'State of Cambodia' and, of course, Khieu Samphan himself, representing the Khmer Rouge. In the picture everybody exudes a sense of relief, bonhomie and optimism; everyone is smiling, but no one more than Khieu Samphan.

Khieu Seng Kim was a child in 1950, when his brother, recently graduated from the Lycée Sisowath, left for Paris on a scholarship. By the time he returned with his Doctorate from the Sorbonne, eight years later, Khieu Seng Kim was fourteen, and the memory of going to Pochentong airport to receive his older brother stayed fresh in his mind. 'We were very poor then,' he said, 'and we couldn't afford to greet him with garlands and a crown of flowers, like well-off people do. We just embraced and hugged and all of us had tears flowing down our cheeks.'

In those days, in Cambodia, a doctorate from France was a guarantee of a high-level job in the government, a sure means of ensuring entry into the country's privileged classes. Their mother wanted nothing less for herself and her family. She had struggled against poverty most of her life; her husband, a magistrate, had died early, leaving her five children to bring up on her own. But when her son refused to accept any of the lucrative offers that came his way despite her entreaties, once again she had to start selling vegetables to keep the family going. Khieu Seng Kim remembers seeing his adored brother — the brilliant economist with his degree from the Sorbonne — sitting beside his mother, helping her with her roadside stall.

In the mean while, Khieu Samphan taught in a school, founded an influential left-wing journal and gradually rose to political prominence. He even served in Sihanouk's cabinet for a while, and with his success the family's situation eased a little.

And then came the day in 1967 when he melted into the jungle.

Khieu Seng Kim remembers the day well: it was Monday, 24 April 1967. His mother served dinner at seven-thirty and the two of them sat at the dining table and waited for Khieu Samphan to arrive: he always came home at about that time. They stayed there till eleven, without eating, listening for every footstep and every sound; then his mother broke down and began to cry. She cried all night, 'like a child who has lost its mother'.

At first they thought that Khieu Samphan had been arrested. They had good reason to, for Prince Sihanouk had made a speech two days before, denouncing Khieu Samphan and two close friends of his, the brothers Hu Nim and Hou Yuon. But no arrest was announced, and nor was there any other news the next day.

Khieu Seng Kim became a man possessed: he could not believe that the brother he worshipped would abandon his family; at that time he was their only means of support. He travelled all over the country, visiting friends and relatives, asking if they had any news of his brother. Nobody could tell him anything: it was only much later that he learnt that Khieu Samphan had been smuggled out of the city in a farmer's cart the evening he failed to show up for dinner.

He never saw him again.

Eight years later, in 1975, when the first Khmer Rouge cadres marched into Phnom Penh, Khieu Seng Kim went rushing out into the streets and threw himself upon them, crying: 'My brother is Khieu Samphan, my brother is your leader'. They looked at him as though he were insane. 'The Revolution doesn't recognize families', they said, brushing him off. He was driven out of the city with his wife and children and made to march to a work-site just like everybody else.

Like most other evacuees Khieu Seng Kim drifted back towards Phnom Penh in 1979, after the Pol Pot regime had been overthrown by the Vietnamese invasion. He began working in a factory, but within a few months it came to be known that he knew French and had worked as a journalist before the Revolution. The new government contacted him and invited him to take up a job as a journalist. He refused; he didn't want to be compromised or associate himself with the government in any way. Instead, he worked with the Department of Archaeology for a while as a restorer, and then took a teaching job at the School of Fine Arts.

'For that they're still suspicious of me', he said, with a wry smile. 'Even now. That's why I live in a place like this, while everyone in the country is getting rich.'

He smiled and lit a cigarette; he seemed obscurely pleased at the thought of being excluded and pushed on to the edges of the wilderness that had claimed his brother decades ago. It never seemed to have occurred to him to reflect that there was probably no other country on earth where the brother of a man who had headed a genocidal regime would actually be invited to accept a job by the government that followed.

I liked Khieu Seng Kim, I liked his quirky younger-brotherishness. For his sake I wished his mother were still alive — that indomitable old woman who had spread out her mat and started selling vegetables on the street when she realized that her eldest son would have no qualms about sacrificing his entire family on the altar of his idealism. She would have reminded Khieu Seng Kim of a few home truths.

14

Khieu Samphan talked very little about his student days upon his return from France. He did however tell one story that imprinted itself vividly on the fourteen-year-old boy's mind. It had to do with an old friend, Hou Yuon.

Hou Yuon was initiated into radical politics at about the same time as Khieu Samphan and Pol Pot; they all attended the same study groups in Paris; they did Party work together in Phnom Penh in the 1960s, and all through the desperate years of the early '70s they fought together, shoulder-to-shoulder, in conditions of the most extreme hardship, with thousands of tons of bombs raining down on them. So closely were Khieu Samphan and Hou Yuon linked, that along with a third friend, Hu Nim, they became a collective legend, known as the Three Ghosts.

Khieu Samphan's acquaintance with Hou Yuon dated back to their schooldays at the Lycée Sisowath in Phnom Penh. Their friendship was sealed in Paris in the 1950s and it was the subject of the story Khieu Samphan told his brother on his return.

Once, at a Cambodian gathering in Paris, Hou Yuon made a speech in which he criticized the corruption and venality of Prince Sihanouk's regime. He was overheard by an official and soon afterwards his government scholarship was suspended for a year. Since Khieu Samphan was known to be a particular friend of his, his scholarship was suspended too.

To support themselves the two men began to sell bread. They would study during the day, and at night they would walk around the city hawking long loaves of French bread. With the money they earned, they paid for their upkeep and bought books; the loaves they couldn't sell they ate. It was a hard way to earn money, Khieu Samphan told his brother, but at the same time it was also oddly exhilarating. Walking down those lamplit streets, late at night, talking to each other, it was as though he and Hou Yuon somehow managed to leave behind the night-time of the spirit that had befallen them in Paris. They would walk all night long, with the fragrant, crusty loaves over their shoulders, looking into the windows of cafes and restaurants, talking about their lives and about the future . . .

Hou Yuon was one of the first to die when the revolution began to devour itself: his moderate views were sharply at odds with the ultra-radical, collectivist ideology of the ruling group. He disappeared in 1975, soon after the Khmer Rouge took power. He is said to have been assassinated on the orders of the party's leadership. The other member of the trio, Hu Nim, served briefly as Minister of Information. Then on 10 April 1977 he was taken into 'Interrogation Centre S–21' — the torture chambers at Tuol Sleng in Phnom Penh: his picture hangs there still.

No matter how well one prepares oneself for Tuol Sleng, one is caught unawares: the horror of it surpasses anything the mind can envisage unaided. This is due partly to the incongruity of the setting — a residential neighbourhood of small bungalows — and partly because of the unexpected appearance of the buildings: solid, three-storeyed schoolhouses, painted a reassuring municipal yellow. They are school buildings of a kind familiar not just in Cambodia, but in India or Bangladesh or Egypt — buildings with large, airy, blackboarded classrooms, in which children chant their multiplication tables sitting at long wooden desks.

The prisoners slept in tiny cubicles which they built themselves, inside the classrooms. The cubicles are made of crude bricks, slapped inexpertly together, with thick scabs of cement oozing out of the cracks. They are no wider than narrow camp-beds and they are built flush against the walls, like rat-traps pushed up against a grate. In each there is a dented, gunmetal-grey canister with a hinged lid, which the prisoners used for their excrement. The metal excrement-canisters are wedged between the bars of the school's windows, silhouetted, in their unspeakable desolation, against the brilliant green light that pours in from the playground outside.

Notices hang on the walls, with instructions and warnings for the prisoners. Some have been translated for the benefit of the Museum's visitors. That grand old eighteenth-century word 'Revolution', with all its magical potency, its promise of freedom, brotherhood and modernity, features prominently, but in inexplicable configurations. Amongst the many exhortations and warnings that instruct prisoners not to cry out loud during interrogation and so on, there is one that reads, 'Don't be a fool or you are a chap who betrays the Revolution'.

Khieu Samphan was head of state when his old comrades were executed for betraying the Revolution. He is believed to have played an important role in planning the mass purges of that period.

For Khieu Samphan and Pol Pot, the deaths of Hou Yuon, Hu Nim and the thousands of others who were executed in torture chambers and execution grounds, were not a contradiction but rather a proof of their own idealism and ideological purity. Terror was essential to their exercise of power. It was an integral part not merely of their coercive machinery, but of the moral order on which they built their regime; a part whose best description still lies in the line that Büchner, most prescient of playwrights, gave to Robespierre (a particular hero of Pol Pot's) — 'Terror is an emanation of virtue'.

15

Those who were there then say there was a moment of epiphany in Phnom Penh in 1988. It occurred at a quiet, relatively obscure event: a festival when classical Cambodian music and dance were performed for the first time since the Revolution.

Dancers and musicians from all over the country travelled to Phnom Penh for the festival. Proeung Chhieng, one of the best-known dancers and choreographers in the country, was one of those who made the journey: he came to Phnom Penh from Kompong Thom where he had helped assemble a small troupe of dancers after the fall of Democratic Kampuchea. He himself had trained at the palace since his childhood, specializing in the role of Hanuman, the monkey-god of the Ramayana epic, a part that is one of the glories of Khmer dance, combining athleticism, mime and rhythm with extraordinary fluency. This training proved instrumental in Proeung Chhieng's survival: his expertise in clowning and mime helped him persuade the interrogators at his labour camp that he was an illiterate lunatic.

At the festival he met many fellow-students and teachers for the first time after the Revolution: 'We cried and laughed while we looked around to see who were the others who had survived. We would shout with joy: "You are still alive!" and then we would cry thinking of someone who had died.'

The performers were dismayed when they began preparing for the performance: large quantities of musical instruments, costumes and masks had been destroyed over the last few years. They had to improvise new costumes to perform in; instead of rich silks and brocades they used thin calico, produced by a government textile factory. The theatre they were to perform in, the Bassac, was in relatively good shape, but there was a crisis of electricity at the time, and the lighting was dim and unreliable.

But people flocked to the theatre the day the festival began. Onesta Carpene, a Catholic relief worker from Italy was one of the handful of foreigners then living in Phnom Penh. She was astonished at the response: the city was in a shambles; there was debris everywhere, spilling out of the houses, on to the pavements, the streets were jammed with pillaged cars, there was no money and very little food — 'I could not believe that in a situation like that people would be thinking of music and dance'. But still they came pouring in, and the theatre was filled far beyond its capacity. It was very hot inside.

Eva Mysliwiec, who had arrived recently to set up a Quaker relief mission, was one of the few foreigners present at that first performance. When the first musicians came onstage she heard sobs all around her. Then, when the dancers appeared, in their shabby, hastily-made costumes, suddenly, everyone was crying: old people, young people, soldiers, children — 'you could have sailed out of there in a boat'.

The people who were sitting next to her said: 'We thought everything was lost, that we would never hear our music again, never see our dance'. They could not stop crying; people wept through the entire length of the performance.

It was a kind of rebirth: a moment when the grief of survival became indistinguishable from the joy of living.

Notes

The account of the royal dance troupe's visit to France with King Sisowath is based on reports in *Le Petit Provençal, Le Petit Marseillais*, and *Le Figaro*; on the *Rapport-Gènèral, Exposition Coloniale Nationale de Marseille, 15 Avril–18 Novembre 1906* (1907), and its accompanying volume, *La Chambre de Commerce de Marseille et l'Exposition Coloniale de 1906* (1908), published by the Chamber of Commerce, Marseille; and on the following letters and documents in the Archives d'Outre–Mer at Aix-en-Provence: Résident-Supérieur in Phnom Penh to Hanoi, 30 May 1905 (re. princes' scholarships to study in France) (GGI 2576); Governor-General to the Minister of Colonies in Paris, 5 April 1906 (GGI 5822); report, F. Gautret, July 1906 (GGI 6643); Minister of Colonies to F. Gautret, Paris, 18 July 1906 (GGI 6643); *Fête du 5 Juillet, 1906, en l'honneur de SM le Roi du Cambodge . . .* (Ministry of Colonies, 1906); F. Gautret, to the Governor-General, Hanoi, 20 August 1906, Saigon (GGI 6643); itinerary, *Sejour de Sa Majestè Sisowath, Roi du Cambodge en France* (GGI 6643); Résident-Supérieur to Governor-General, 18 January 1907, containing a French translation of the royal proclamation on the King's voyage, issued under the signatures of King Sisowath and five ministers (GGI 5822); Minister Thiounn to Résident-Supérieur, 9 July 1907 (GGI 2576); correspondence between the Cour des Comptes, Paris, Saigon and Phnom Penh on expenses of the royal entourage (1901–11), including Minister Thiounn's response (13 August 1910) (GGI 15606). The quotations in section 10 are from *Rodin et l'Extrême Orient* (Musée Rodin, Paris, 1979), and from Frederic V. Grunefeld's, *Rodin; A Biography* (Henry Holt & Co., New York, 1987). Biographical and other details on Cambodian politics and history are mainly from Milton E. Osborne's, *The French Presence in Cochinchina and Cambodia: Rule and Response (1859–1950)* (Cornell Univ. Press, Ithaca, 1969); David Chandler's *Brother Number One; A Political Biography of Pol Pot* (Westview, Oxford, 1992); Ben Kiernan's, *How Pol Pot Came to Power: A History of Communism in Kampuchea, 1930–75* (Verso, London, 1985), and Elizabeth Becker's, *When the War was Over: the Voices of Cambodia's Revolution and its People* (Simon & Schuster, New York, 1986).

The author gratefully acknowledges the help of the staff of the Archives d'Outre–Mer in Aix-en-Provence and of the following individuals: Christian Oppetit, Conservator of the archives of the Département des Bouches-du-Rhône; Annie Terrier, Christianne Besse, Eva Mysliwiec, Chanthou Boua, Tan Sotho, Choup Sros, Kim Rath, Bill Lobban, Mr T.P. Seetharam, Col Suresh Nair and Mrs Pushpa Nair.

2

Stories in Stones

From the minute I first entered Angkor Wat I found myself awash in stories. I was puzzled by this in the beginning, but now, looking back, several months later, it seems to me that there was something inevitable in it. For above all Angkor Wat is a monument to the power of the story.

This is true in a perfectly literal sense: with every step a visitor takes in this immense twelfth-century Cambodian temple he finds himself moving counters in a gigantic abacus of story-telling. The device is a vast one — it is said to be the largest single religious edifice in the world — and it provides its own setting as well as a cast of galactic dimensions. The setting is Mt Meru, the sacred mountain of ancient Indian myth, whose seven carefully graded tiers provide the blueprint for the temple's form. The cast is the entire pantheon of gods, deities, sages and prophets with which that cosmos is peopled.

But no story, no matter how loftily cosmic, is ever entirely free of its origins: as with all the best stories, this one too is partly an autobiography, an allegory about its own authorship. The chief protagonists in this instance are such imperial figures as King Suryavarman II, who was mainly responsible for building Angkor Wat, and Jayavarman VII, the megalomaniacal ruler who ruined his empire in trying to create the nearby complex of Angkor Thom. But secure in its unyielding vastness, the temple stands guard over many other kinds of autobiography as well.

I heard one such from a Cambodian conservation worker called Kong Sarith. One afternoon he was telling me about some of the legends depicted in Angkor Wat's magnificent bas-reliefs: the primal myth of the churning of the Sea of Milk; the legend of Vishnu in his tortoise-avatar; of the doomed Abhimanyu, trapped in a battle formation that he had learnt to enter but not escape; of the death-god Yama ruling over his tormented shades. The stories were all familiar to me, of course, some in the misty way of tales told by a grandmother; others in the manner of texts, learned under the threat of a tutor's cane and quickly forgotten. But for Kong Sarith the stories were vividly alive; he told them in the confiding, urgent way in which people describe their neighbours' overheard quarrels. He was a thin, slight man, in his early forties, with a wispy, incongruously villainous-looking moustache. He spoke fluent English, in a rapid, gravelly voice that sometimes broke into a hacking laugh. His hands were never without a cigarette and while he spoke he seemed to paint the air with its glowing tip, conjuring up visions with curls of blue smoke.

Then, talking of the intricate iconography of those sculpted panels, he turned a page, and we were suddenly in an altogether different kind of story.

If Sarith's story took me by surprise it was because it was so unexpected.

For in the time I'd spent in Cambodia, I had made a discovery about Angkor Wat: I had discovered that its place in the world rests upon a kind of paradox. For many people, around the globe, Angkor Wat is a uniquely powerful symbol of the romance of lost civilizations; of ancient glory, devoured by time. But for Cambodia it serves as a no less vivid symbol of modernity.

Images of Angkor Wat are so common in Cambodia, so inescapable that after a while they become an assault upon the visitor's senses; the visual equivalent of radio-music played on public loudspeakers. There are so many of them, everywhere, that at first the images appear to be omnipresent, ubiquitous. But the impression is misleading; the images are *not* ubiquitous — in fact they are never where one expects. Angkor Wat is, for example, undisputedly a temple, yet it never figures in anything to do with religion, or indeed in any context that might be called 'traditional' or old-fashioned. Its likeness appears instead on certain factory-produced commodities, like beer; it is stamped on uniforms, civil and military; it figures on the logos of large corporations, like banks: indeed, the erstwhile Kampuchea Airlines even succeeded in transforming this most earthbound of structures into a symbol of flight, by lending it a pair of wings.

Most of all, Angkor Wat belongs on flags — flags of the country and flags of political parties. Cambodia has been torn between factions for decades; no country on earth has witnessed more bitter or more violent political strife. Yet, although the country's flag has changed with every new regime over the last forty years, there has always been one constant in its design: it has never ceased to bear an image of Angkor.

Several of the parties that contested the 1994 UN-sponsored elections contrived somehow to work Angkor Wat into their flags: it was as though their claim to govern depended on it. One of the oddest of those flags belonged to a small party founded by an expatriate Cambodian businessman from California. The party was called 'Republic Democracy Khmer', and its flag looked very much like the Stars and Stripes except that in place of the Stars, it featured a five-towered image of Angkor Wat.

Flags, uniforms, banks, airlines, beer: it isn't hard to predict yet-unrealized continuations of the series — cigarettes, shaving cream, fertilizers, personal computers, assault rifles and so on. Temples and monasteries do not figure in this series and, indeed, nothing in Cambodia is more innocent of references to Angkor than the Buddhist Wats, or pagodas, which are the country's most prominent landmarks, in town and village alike. These graceful, richly ornamented shrines, with their sinuous woodwork, are about as different from the massive, obscurely vegetal forms of Angkor Wat as any that could be imagined.

Nowhere is this contrast better illustrated than in Angkor Wat itself. Hidden behind rows of trees, in the temple's first great courtyard, at a discreet distance from the flagstoned causeway that leads into the inner section of the monument, are two modest little pagodas. Tourists and archaeologists head straight down the causeway towards the temple's colonnaded galleries, armed with their cameras and calipers; local people, pilgrims, religious supplicants and so on veer off towards the Buddhist shrines, bearing offerings and flowers.

One morning, electing to follow the pilgrims for a change, I made my way to one of those pagodas.

The shrine, with its brightly-coloured, larger-than-life-size image of the Buddha, was tended by an elderly Buddhist monk: a tall, acquiline man whose saffron robes hung upon his skeletal limbs like sheets on a wire fence. Several families were sitting on the scrubbed tile floor of the shrine when I arrived. Some had come in share-taxis and others had bicycled all the way from the town of Siem Reap, several miles away. They were all waiting to be blessed. The monk chanted prayers for each group in turn, and then led them outside and drenched them in holy water.

When my turn came, I asked if he would mind talking to me, through an interpreter. He agreed readily, but with the stipulation that the conversation would have to be interrupted for those of his flock who were in a particular hurry.

He was known as the Ven. Luong Chun, he said, and he had lived on the premises of Angkor Wat most of his life. He had entered the monastery at Angkor Wat in his adolescence, and he remembered a time when the layout of the temple's grounds was quite different. At that time a pagoda sat directly in front of the collonaded galleries of the temple (it can be seen clearly in turn-of-the century photographs — an untidy, thatch-roofed structure, flanking the great flagstoned causeway). His grandfather, who had spent some time in the monastery too, had told him the story of how the pagoda came to be moved.

The French archaeologists who were restoring Angkor Wat had decided that the pagoda had to go: an actual, functioning shrine had no place in their pristine vision of the temple. They wanted it to be shunted off the premises altogether, but the monks had resisted. There had been a Buddhist monastery within Angkor for centuries and they could not conceive of abandoning the site altogether.

Eventually the seniormost monk had led a delegation to the then ruler of Cambodia, King Monivong (Prince Sihanouk's predecessor on the throne). At the King's intercession the monks were allowed to remain within Angkor Wat, but in purdah, as it were — on the condition that they moved the pagoda off its old site and rebuilt it at a suitable distance.

The Ven. Luong Chun had himself worked for the French archaeologists as a boy. Along with hundreds of others, he had been hired to crush stones from Angkor Wat and Angkor Thom, so that roads could be built to connect the monuments to Siem Reap.

The Ven. Luong Chun was living in Angkor Wat in April 1975 when the Khmer Rouge seized power. There were about four hundred monks in the monastery at the time: several of them were killed, some right on the threshold of the pagoda. He, along with the others, was taken away to a work-camp some distance away. He was stripped of his monk's robes which were cut up and made into trousers, and he spent the three years of the 'Pol Pot time' working in the ricefields.

In January 1979, after the Khmer Rouge had been driven from power by the Vietnamese invasion, it was announced at his work-camp that Angkor Wat was badly in need of cleaning and people who were familiar with it were welcome to go back. He set off for the temple soon afterwards and for the next two years he and a few other monks tried to clear the monument as best they could.

In tending the temple during that time the Ven. Luong Chun was doing what monks like him had done for centuries: there is evidence that monks continued to live in Angkor Wat even after the Angkorian period, when the complex fell into general decline. Thus the most powerful of the myths that surround Angkor — the legend of its accidental discovery by the nineteenth-century French explorer Henri Mouhot — is no more and no less true than any of the others inscribed upon the temple. For if it is true that Angkor was already well-known to the Buddhist Sangha and to the nobility of Cambodia and Thailand — not as a fetish, perhaps, but in the quotidian way in which medieval monuments are usually absorbed into living history — it is also true that Mouhot and the French did indeed make a discovery. They discovered a mirror for themselves: of the Imperial State, *l'Etat*, in all its power and splendour.

The story that the Ven. Luong Chun heard from his grandfather was one version of the reinvention of Angkor in that image. The process began by separating the monument, so far as possible, from the untidy uses of its present-day inhabitants, and went on to 'restore' it by applying the most advanced scientific methods available.

The story is a familiar one, for in this century many other parts of the world have seen their present being technologically and symbolically superseded by the relicts of their past. But in Cambodia the process went further than elsewhere. For an entire generation of Cambodians, including politicians as different in ideology as Prince Sihanouk, Son Sann and Pol Pot, Angkor Wat became a symbol of the modernizing nation-state. It became the opposite of itself: an icon that represented a break with the past — a token of the country's belonging, not within the medieval, but rather the contemporary world.

Thus the beer, banks, airlines and, of course, flags.

Unlike the Ven. Luong Chun, my newfound acquaintance, the chain-smoking Kong Sarith, had no previous connection with Angkor, although he now had a job there. Sarith spent his childhood at the other end of the country, in a small village near Phnom Penh, where his father ran a business. After finishing school he moved to the city and joined the Faculty of Law and Economics at the University of Phnom Penh.

He began college in the midst of a civil war, while the city was under fire from the Khmer Rouge and parts of the country were being subjected to saturation-bombing by

American B–52s. He was in his second year when the Khmer Rouge entered Phnom Penh and began the forcible evacuation of the city. He was moved out on the second day of the evacuation: first to the city of Battambang, and then on to Sisophon, a small town in the north-west. From there, along with a group of other 'new people', he was marched to a labour camp, a few miles away.

Soon after they arrived at the camp, Khmer Rouge cadres began to interrogate them about their lives. Unlike some of the other inmates, Sarith realized early on that to tell the truth about a background like his was as good as signing a death warrant. He thought the matter through very carefully and in the end he made up a story in which he cast himself as a waiter in a roadside eating-place in Phnom Penh.

He spent a lot of time thinking about his story, especially at night. The daytimes were all right; you were so busy in the rice-fields you never had a moment to think — you felt relatively safe during the day. It was the nights that were really terrifying: 'the time of the death-god Yama'. That was when they came for you; you would lie still inside your mosquito-net and listen to their footsteps as they went over to some other bed and led someone away. You wouldn't ask; you wouldn't look; but sometimes, in the morning, you would see a mound of earth where the victim had been buried.

Sarith spent a lot of time, during those long nights, thinking his story through. And just as well, for one day, while he was out in the rice-fields, the cadres pulled him out and took him to meet a new interrogator — someone who looked vaguely familiar.

Sarith told his usual story, but when he finished the interrogator asked: 'All right — which restaurant did you work in then?'

Sarith had his answer ready, and he gave it to him, pat: it was the name of an establishment that he had known well, having frequented it as a student.

His interrogator started when he heard the name and suddenly Sarith knew why he looked familiar. 'I used to eat there all the time', he said. 'I knew all the waiters; I don't remember you.'

Sarith had to think on his feet. 'Which years did you eat there?' he asked.

The man mentioned some dates and Sarith answered immediately: 'At that time I was working inside, in the kitchen. That's why you didn't see me. It was only later that the owner told me to start waiting on the tables.'

His interrogator didn't quite buy the story, but he couldn't knock it down either. He said: 'All right, if you really worked in the kitchen there, let's see how hard you can work here.' After that they made him get out of bed at half-past two in the morning to wash dishes in the work-camp's communal kitchen. And somehow he managed to carry it off, as if he had done nothing else all his life, although there were times when he thought he would die of exhaustion.

In 1978, shortly before the regime collapsed, he was forcibly married off, along with seven other couples. His wife was a woman from Phnom Penh and he had never met her before. Marriage was the last thing on his mind at the time and he didn't want to marry her. Yet the marriage lasted and they went on to have four children: 'After suffering through so much together, we could not leave each other.'

Around 3 January 1979, when the Vietnamese army was approaching Sisophon, the people in Sarith's camp were herded together and told that the 'new people' could leave next morning if they wanted to, and that they would be given a little rice to take with them. Two of the inmates made the mistake of cheering: that night they were led out to the cassava fields and clubbed to death.

The next morning they were set free and handed milk-tins filled with rice. Sarith left the camp with his wife and began walking towards Siem Reap, with the intention of going on to Phnom Penh to find his family. On the way they fell in with some other people from their camp and they decided to go on together; they slept beside the road, at night, and boiled their rice in empty milk-tins, over open fires.

They walked into the town of Siem Reap on the night of 21 January. The next morning, led by a member of their group — a young woman — Sarith and a few others began walking towards Angkor. The woman who led them there had been an inmate in the same camp as Sarith, and in a way they were familiar with each other. But on the way to Angkor, Sarith made a discovery that astonished him: the woman revealed herself to be an archaeologist, and said she had once known the temple well. Like Sarith himself, she had been so successful in disguising her identity at the work-camp that he scarcely knew whether or not to believe her now.

Sarith had never been to Angkor Wat before: he had heard about it of course, and seen pictures and so on, but still, seeing it before his eyes now, he was dumbstruck. The monument was completely overgrown: in the last few years the jungle had marched in and claimed it for its own, but the luxuriance of the vegetation only served to highlight the majesty of the structure.

They made their way very slowly down the flagstoned causeway. Once they got to the colonnaded galleries they were filled with curiosity at the sight of the mossy bas-reliefs. They sat down right there, on the stone floor of the gallery, and asked the woman to tell them about the legends depicted on the panels.

'You must remember,' said Sarith, 'for years we had seen nothing but hunger, death and famine.' Now, they would not let the woman stop; they listened entranced as she recounted those old, old stories. Slowly they worked their way around the vast galleries, listening to the stories over and over again.

'By the end of the day', said Sarith, 'I knew I could not leave, I said: I will spend the rest of my life here, in Angkor Wat.'

That was in January 1979. He went away for a while in 1981, cycling all the way to Phnom Penh, to look for his parents. He found, as he had feared, that they were dead. As soon as he could, he turned and headed back to that great, grey mountain of stone that had absorbed him into its teeming worlds.

3

At Large in Burma

Like many Indians, I grew up on stories of other countries: places my parents and relatives had lived in or visited before the birth of the Republic of India, in 1947. To me, the most intriguing of these stories were those that my family carried out of Burma. I suspect that this was partly because Burma had become a kind of lost world in the early '60s, when I was old enough to listen to my relatives' stories. It was in 1962 that General Ne Win, the man who would be Burma's longtime dictator, seized power in a coup. Almost immediately, he slammed the shutters and switched off the lights: Burma became the dark house of the neighbourhood, huddled behind an impenetrable, overgrown fence. It was to remain shuttered for almost three decades.

In retrospect, I am astonished by the degree to which the Ne Win regime succeeded in cutting the country off, even from the attention of its immediate neighbours. Burma is one of the larger countries in South-east Asia, with a land area considerably greater than that of Thailand and a population of an estimated forty-six million. Its border with India is hundreds of miles long. Calcutta is closer to Burma's principal urban centres, Rangoon and Mandalay, than it is to New Delhi. Yet, while other neighbouring countries —

Pakistan, Bangladesh, Sri Lanka — figured in our newspapers to the point of obsession, Burma was scarcely mentioned. In defiance of the laws of proximity, General Ne Win was able to render his country invisible to both its neighbours and the world at large.

In my family, memories of Burma were kept alive by an old connection, and last December, on travelling to Rangoon, I found a trace of that connection in a small, nondescript Durga temple in the commercial centre of the city. The temple stands on a broad, straight road that was once known as Spark Street; it is now called Bo Aung Kyaw Street. This part of Rangoon was planned and built by British engineers in the late nineteenth century, and Spark Street still has a dark, gaslit Victorian feel to it.

The temple on Spark Street is merely a hall on the ground floor of an old apartment building. It was built in 1887 and has served ever since as a community centre for Bengali immigrants. I had heard about the temple as a child, from an aunt who had married into a wealthy Bengali family that had settled in Burma. My aunt's husband ran a prosperous timber business. He was nicknamed the Prince because of his extravagant tastes. My aunt and the Prince left Burma in 1942, in the last, panic-sticken weeks before the Japanese Army marched into Rangoon. They managed to bribe their way on to a ship that was sailing for Calcutta.

The couple settled in Calcutta, and the Prince went back into the timber business. He was a distinguished-looking man, aquiline and ruddy-cheeked, always dressed in a starched cotton kurta and dhoti. In my earliest memories, he is a figure of truly princely munificence, driving up in his chauffeured Studebaker to sweep his relatives off to the most expensive shops in the city. This was not the way people did things in Calcutta; it was the Burmese side of him, and, in the semi-socialist India of that time, it couldn't last. He began to slide down the economic scale, slowly at first and then with gathering speed. By the time I was old enough to talk to him, his cars were gone, and he was living in a small fourth-floor flat in a part of Calcutta where almost everyone was a refugee from somewhere or other; he just happened to be from further away than most.

The flat was crammed with books — from Mickey Spillane to Knut Hamsun. The Prince read voraciously and eclectically, mainly in English — a language I never heard him speak. When I went to visit him, he would lay aside his books and talk of Burma.

'It was a golden land', he would say. 'The richest country in Asia except for Japan. There are no people on earth to compare with the Burmese — so generous, so hospitable, so kind to strangers. No one goes hungry in Burma: you just have to ask and someone will feed you.'

In college, I discovered that the picture was not quite so simple. Indians had settled in Burma in large numbers in the late nineteenth century, after the British completed their conquest of the country. Indians had occupied a disproportionate number of government posts, and Indian merchants and moneylenders had come to dominate crucial sectors of the country's economy. I argued with the Prince. 'But Indians were bitterly resented in Burma, weren't they?' I'd say. 'Burmese nationalism practically started with anti-Indian riots.'

He acknowledged this with a nod and a shrug. 'But that's just one part of the story', he'd say. 'There was a lot of friendship, too.' Then his eyes would light up again: 'Ah, but it was a golden land. . . .' It is impossible, I suspect, to imagine oneself being resented by a place to which one has given such unreserved love.

Neither the Prince nor my aunt ever returned to Burma, but my father, who had visited them there, went back once. The year was 1945, and he was an officer serving in the Allied Fourteenth Army. As the Allied forces advanced on Rangoon from the north, my father found himself both amazed and appalled by the scale of the destruction around him. The British had adopted a scorched-earth policy when they withdrew from Burma in 1942, demolishing bridges, setting fire to oil fields, and blocking the Irrawaddy's navigation channels with scuttled ships. Three years later, the retreating Japanese had reciprocated, destroying all that was left of Burma's infrastructure. 'When buffaloes fight', goes a Burmese proverb, 'the grass gets trampled.' By the end of the war, after two bitterly fought campaigns, Burma was a devastated country.

My father found Rangoon virtually unrecognizable, but on making his way to Spark Street he discovered that the temple had survived, and he was able to trace a few distant relatives who had remained in the neighbourhood. They would have starved, they told him later, but for the Army rations he steered their way.

On the evening of my visit, the temple was all but empty: a handful of elderly men were seated around a table in the neon-lit hall. I went up to them and earned a warm welcome by mentioning the Prince's family name. Soon, as I sat with them around the table, the conversation turned to pre-war Burma, and I found myself listening to echoes of the Prince's voice, intoning the very same words: 'A golden land, the richest country in Asia, the envy of its neighbours, the kindest, most hospitable people on earth — even now, when everything is so scarce . . .'

How did it all go wrong? I asked. Fifty years earlier, Burma had been the most developed country in the region, with an impressive agricultural surplus and a superabundance of natural resources — oil, timber, minerals. It had had an important petroleum industry, a highly educated population, almost universal adult literacy, a lively independent press, a rich literary culture, and a framework of democratic institutions. Now it was one of the most impoverished countries in the world's fastest-developing region, one of the United Nations' ten least developed nations on earth, and a byword for repression, xenophobia, and civil abuse. How could any country travel so far back so fast?

The man seated next to me tapped my arm. He was well over seventy, a thin, upright man with a thatch of white hair. I shall call him Mr Bose. Mr Bose led me to the temple's entrance and pointed across the street, toward the dark, unlit compound of the Secretariat Building, a sprawling complex of decaying red brick offices, built by the British at the turn of the century. 'Do you see that veranda there?' he said, pointing to one on a second-floor walkway. 'That was where Burma's future ended. Do you see that door? It leads to the room where General Aung San was assassinated, on 19 July 1947. I was just down the corridor — I saw his body lying there.'

I had often heard my father speak of General Aung San: he had met him once at an Army barracks in Rangoon during the war. General Aung San had said very little — he was famously a man of few words — but he had made a powerful impression on everyone present. He was twenty-nine years old at the time, a strikingly good-looking young man, with high cheekbones, a receding hairline, and a good-humoured twinkle in his eye.

Despite his youth, Aung San was the country's acknowledged leader, the hero of its independence movement. A few years before, as a young student-politician, he had fled from British-ruled Burma and received military training from the

Japanese. He was instrumental in organizing a militia of Burmese nationals in Thailand. In 1942, he marched back across the border at the head of the Burma Independence Army, accompanying the invading Japanese forces. Later, increasingly distrustful of the Japanese, he and his soldiers switched loyalties and joined the Allies. At the end of the war, it was widely believed that General Aung San would assume Burma's leadership once the British granted the country its independence, in 1948.

Aung San was by birth a Burman, and thus a member of the country's largest ethnic group. The Burmans are predominantly Buddhist, and form two-thirds of the country's population. There are four sizeable minorities — the Karen, the Rakhine, the Shan, and the Mon — and many smaller groups. Some are Buddhist, and are linked with the people of neighbouring Thailand. Others, such as the Kachin, the Karen, and the Karenni, include Christians, mainly from families that were converted by American Baptist missionaries in the nineteenth century. And in the west there is also a substantial Muslim population.

What these different minorities have had in common, historically, is a fear of being dominated by the Burmans. Aung San, uniquely, was able to transcend this historical mistrust of Burman politicians: it probably helped that he was married to a Christian, Daw Khin Kyi, although he himself was a Buddhist.

In April 1947, Burma's colonial administration held elections to choose the government that would assume power when the country became independent. Aung San led his party, the Anti-Fascist People's Freedom League, to a resounding electoral victory. He was thirty-two; he had been married nearly five years and had fathered three children. The youngest, Suu Kyi, was two years old.

The events of 19 July 1947 were fresh in Mr Bose's memory, kept alive by years of telling and retelling. He was then working as a clerical superintendent in the colonial administration. His job required him to sit at a desk in a large hall, overseeing a team of clerks. General Aung San and his kitchen cabinet were meeting in a room down the corridor; Mr Bose knew that room well, for he often delivered files there.

Mr Bose was sitting at his desk at ten-fifteen on the morning of 19 July when he heard an earsplitting noise. He looked up to find himself staring at a roomful of startled clerks. Then he heard feet thudding along the corridor and down the stairs. It took a moment before he realized that the earsplitting noise had been gunfire. By the time Mr Bose reached the door, a crowd had gathered there. The room was full of smoke. Standing on tiptoe, he counted nine bodies inside, some sprawled on the floor, some slumped over a table. Six members of the cabinet had died with General Aung San. They were among the country's most respected politicians, and included some of its most important minority leaders. Mr Bose looked down and saw a thin trickle of blood winding past his feet.

Mr Bose learned that a group of men dressed in battle fatigues had driven into the Secretariat compound in two jeeps, through the entrance on Dalhousie Street. They had run directly to the cabinet room, carrying guns; they had known exactly where to go. The soldiers ran back the way they had come, jumped into their jeeps, and drove away through the same gate. That was the last that was ever heard of them, although several suspects were rounded up and a right-wing politician was later charged with the assassination and hanged.

This is the end, Mr Bose thought as he stood in the

corridor, looking into the bloody room. Nothing will ever be the same again.

'Can you imagine the consequences in India or China if this had happened to Nehru and his Cabinet or to Mao and the Politburo?' Mr Bose said to me. 'That's something you have to remember when you think of Burma.'

The new Union of Burma attained its independence on schedule, in January 1948. U Nu, a trusted friend of Aung San's who had assumed the leadership of the Party after the General's assassination, was sworn in as Burma's first Prime Minister.

Three months later, civil war broke out, with a vast Communist uprising. Serious ethnic insurgencies started the following year, when a group of Karen soldiers seized an armoury on the outskirts of Rangoon and dug themselves in against government troops. Two Karen regiments of the Burma Army then mutinied, and they were soon joined by a regiment of Kachins.

In colonial times, British recruiting policies favoured minority groups over the ethnic Burmans. The British Burma Army was formed largely of units such as the Karen Rifles and the Kachin Rifles. As a result, the civil war began with the insurgents outnumbering government troops, and they made short work of the government's inexperienced, understaffed official Army. They captured Mandalay, Burma's second city, within six weeks, and then advanced on Rangoon, the capital, which was already under siege, caught between Communist insurgents and Karen rebels. A year after independence, the authority of the Burmese government extended no further than the city's outskirts. The administration came to be nicknamed the Rangoon Six-Mile Government. It survived largely because an arms shipment from India arrived just in time to supply the government's troops.

In the following decades, the people of Burma learned to live with quotidian violence on a scale unimaginable elsewhere until the global advent of terrorism. The famously phlegmatic writer Norman Lewis travelled through Burma in 1951 and found that guerrilla warfare had become so widespread as to be commonplace: bridges were demolished within hours of being rebuilt; railway tracks were repaired and blown up at clockwork intervals; trains and riverboats were fired upon with mechanical regularity. 'In the situation of this unfortunate country,' he wrote, 'there is an element of grim Wellsian prediction come to fulfilment.'

General Aung San may indeed have been the only Burmese leader who could have averted the civil war. A few months before his death, he had negotiated a landmark treaty with several minority groups, having been able to persuade them that their rights would be protected in a quasi-federal union. The treaty, known as the Panglong Agreement, laid the groundwork for what could well have been a viable federal union. With General Aung San's assassination, the agreement foundered.

In his death, General Aung San became Burma's most pervasive icon. It is easy to imagine that the people of Rangoon, beset on every side by civil strife, needed a symbol to remind them that Burma was more than a flag and a fantasy — that an eventual Union of Burma was indeed thinkable, even achievable. Aung San became the embodiment of that possibility. For, despite the strains of the civil war, Burma clung fast to its parliamentary constitution: through the next decade, elections were held regularly, and the press flourished.

Then, in 1962, General Ne Win, the chief of the Army, abruptly took control of the government and suspended the constitution. The new regime met with immediate civilian resistance. Students sealed off Rangoon University and declared it a 'fortress of democracy'. The police opened fire, killing an unknown number; blew up the student-union building; and then closed the university. Many students went underground; many fled to insurgent-controlled areas on the border.

Soon after General Ne Win took power, it was announced that the ideology of the new regime was to be 'the Burmese Way to Socialism'. The General had a history of peculiar behaviour, and soon became famous for his tantrums and an obsession with the number nine. He was said by many to be mad, and had undergone psychiatric treatment in Vienna. His professed ideology proved to be no ideology at all, but a bizarre mix of xenophobia and astrology, with a smattering of Marxism. General Ne Win's one claim to legitimacy was a connection to Aung San, who had once been his comrade-in-exile, and the General made the most of the link. As the reality of Burma grew ever more distant from Aung San's vision, his image proliferated: on coins and banknotes, on street corners, in marketplaces.

It takes a military dictator to believe that symbols are inert and can be manipulated at will. Forty years after his assassination, Aung San had his revenge. In a strange, secular reincarnation, his daughter, Suu Kyi, came back to haunt those who had sought to make use of his death. In 1988, when Burma's decades of discontent culminated in an anti-military uprising, Aung San Suu Kyi emerged from obscurity as one of the country's most powerful voices, the personification of Burma's democratic resistance to military rule.

The first time I met Suu Kyi was in 1980, at Oxford, where I was then a graduate student. I had been given a package for her by a mutual friend in New Delhi; Suu Kyi went to school and college in Delhi before going on to Oxford. She still has many friends in India. Her mother served as Burma's Ambassador to India for several years.

In 1980, Suu Kyi was thirty-five, and was leading a life of quiet, exiled domesticity on a leafy street in North Oxford, bringing up two sons, then aged seven and three, and writing occasional articles for scholarly journals.

I saw her next in a magazine photograph, eight years later: she was speaking into a microphone. It was 26 August 1988, and she was addressing a vast crowd in the shadow of the great golden spire of the Shwedagon Pagoda, in Rangoon. She was instantly recognizable and yet utterly transformed.

I learned later that her presence in Burma was largely fortuitous. In the course of a peripatetic life, spent in many countries abroad, Suu Kyi had returned regularly to visit her ageing mother in Rangoon, and news that she had suffered a stroke was what brought Suu Kyi back in 1988.

Mass protests against military rule had started a couple of weeks before Suu Kyi arrived in Rangoon. In March, a brawl in a tea shop provoked a clash between university students and riot police, and forty-one students died of suffocation while being detained in a police van. The students responded by taking to the streets in protest against the regime. The demonstrations continued over several weeks. Three months later, in June, student protests erupted again, eventually forcing the resignation of General Ne Win. The scale of the protests increased after the dictator's departure, culminating in a nationwide general strike on 8 August: in commemoration of this day, many Burmese still refer to the democracy agitation as the Four Eights Movement, because of the date — 8/8/88. Thousands of people — not just students but teachers, monks, children, doctors, and workers of all kind — joined the demonstrations. That day, the Army made its first determined attempt to crush the movement, and hundreds of unarmed demonstrators were shot dead. The killings went on for a week, but demonstrators continued to flood the streets.

Pictures of General Aung San were a prominent feature of the student-led demonstrations. He had himself begun his political career as a student leader, and the generation that formed the nucleus of the democracy movement was quick to lay claim to his legacy. Suu Kyi's family house, on University Avenue, became a centre of political activity, and on 26 August, in her speech at the Shwedagon Pagoda, she announced that she was joining the movement. 'I could not, as my father's daughter, remain indifferent to all that was going on', she told the hundreds of thousands of people who had gathered to listen to her. 'This national crisis could, in fact, be called the second struggle for national independence.'

A bloody dénouement was a few weeks away. On 18 September, a group of senior military officers took over the government. The junta called itself the State Law and Order Restoration Council; it rules under that name to this day, although some of its senior members have changed. In Burma, the regime is universally referred to by the almost comically sinister acronym SLORC. The word is pronounced with an appropriately slurping, swallowing sound — 'like Ian Fleming's SMERSH', as a diplomat once observed.

The junta's first move was to eliminate the democracy movement. Army units took control of the streets, machine-gunning any large gatherings, and arrested hundreds of activists. A mass exodus resulted: as many as six thousand students fled to insurgent-held areas on the border. Many joined the insurgents; some are still fighting.

Once SLORC had secured power, it announced that it

would hold elections. In response, Suu Kyi and her associates formed a political party, the National League for Democracy. Over the next several months, Suu Kyi toured the country, campaigning. She drew vast crowds at every appearance, and her popularity became a matter of increasing concern for the new regime. On 20 July 1989, the day after the forty-second anniversary of her father's death, she was put under house arrest and barred from taking part in the elections. Her disenfranchisement did not have the effect the junta had hoped for. When elections were eventually held, the following year, her party won more than eighty per cent of the seats. Faced with the prospect of being ousted from power, SLORC ignored the result. Suu Kyi was offered safe passage out of the country on the condition that she never return. She chose to remain in Rangoon under house arrest and became the living symbol of Burma's predicament. In 1991, she was awarded the Nobel Peace Prize, but she was unable to collect it: she was still under detention.

Suu Kyi's house arrest ended on 11 July 1995. Within hours of the announcement, a crowd gathered outside her house. She made a brief appearance, but the crowd wanted more. A larger crowd gathered the next day and a still larger one the day after that, waiting in silent vigil until she appeared at the gates. After making such impromptu appearances for several days, Suu Kyi decided that her daily addresses were taking too much of her time, so she resolved to hold regular meetings on weekend afternoons instead. Thus was invented a unique political institution: Suu Kyi's gateside meetings in Rangoon.

Before travelling to Burma, I had often wondered how SLORC had succeeded in keeping its hold on power for the past eight years, despite the overwhelming popular support for Suu Kyi and the National League for Democracy. The answers became evident once I was there. Military rulers in impoverished countries are frequently brutal, but they are rarely able to muster either the resources or the expertise required to operate complex systems of social control. Burma is an exception. Despite the country's meagre resources, its successive military regimes have succeeded in creating systems of surveillance that are unsurpassed in the scope of their intrusiveness.

To take just one example: every household in Burma must register its members with the local authority; no one may spend the night at another household without obtaining permission from the local ward chairman. Members of ethnic minorities frequently have difficulty registering changes in their 'guestlists'. In Rangoon, I met a woman who, after three years of wedlock, still had to queue for weekly permission to stay at her husband's apartment.

References in the press to poverty are automatically censored, and so are references to corruption, bribery, and even disease. 'The censors live in a world of illusion', a well-known writer told me. 'On the one hand, they know everything; they have informers everywhere. They know how much people earn, how much they spend. But in an authoritarian culture people lead two-track lives.'

At the end of our harrowing conversation, I asked, 'What would you write about if there were no censorship?'

He threw up his hands in a gesture of helplessness. He had spent almost ten years in Burma's prisons, most of them in an island concentration camp, where he had had to forage for his food. 'Since 1962, we have lived through the Dark Ages', he said. His voice shook as he tried to control his rage. 'Torture, murder, poverty . . . I have never been able to write about any of these things.'

The country's chief censoring body is the Press Scrutiny Board. Among the items that attracted its ire last year were two magazine covers: one featured a penguin on an ice floe, and the other pictured a young woman seated among fallen flowers; both were interpreted as oblique references to Suu Kyi.

The first time I attended one of Suu Kyi's weekend meetings, in December 1995, I was taken aback by her public manner. I was startled by how much she laughed. At times, she would break up in giggles, with a hand over her mouth; at other times, she would laugh full-throatedly, throwing her head back. I had expected, I suppose, a certain solemnity of demeanour — if for no other reason than merely as an acknowledgement of the atmosphere of intimidation that surrounds those meetings. The people in the crowd didn't seem to care: they laughed with her, uproariously.

The meetings are held at four in the afternoon. Crowds start gathering at midday, and they vary in size from four thousand to ten thousand. Suu Kyi addresses them as she stands at her gate. People sit in orderly rows opposite her, hugging their *longyi*-shrouded knees, while vendors hawk cheroots, betel, and skewers of blackened chicken. Vans, cars, and mini-buses throng the avenue, squeezing slowly through the crowd. The passengers try to look nonchalant, but their composure dissolves once they spot Suu Kyi, and they smile and wave, craning their necks to get a full view. From time to time, intelligence men holding video cameras stand up and pan slowly over the crowd.

The form of the meetings is simple. Suu Kyi answers written questions given to her by members of the crowd. The questions range from matters of food and health to politics and literature. On Sundays, she is joined by at least one senior member of her party, a reminder that the National League for Democracy is a party and not an individual.

University Avenue is a curving, tree-shaded street that skirts the picturesque Inya Lake. Suu Kyi's house, screened by a mass of unkempt greenery, is not visible from the street. When I later walked through the house's blue gates to meet her, I was surprised by how modest and dilapidated the building was: a plain but solid two-storey bungalow, with a portico and veranda overlooking a garden and the lake.

I was shown to a large room on the ground floor. A portrait of her father hung on a flaking, mildewed wall, slightly askew. Close by was an orange banner bearing the symbol of the National League for Democracy — a fighting peacock. Through a barred window, I caught a glimpse of the lake, its sunbathed surface speckled with lotus pads.

When Suu Kyi entered the room, dressed, as usual, in a Burmese sarong, I knew why she had made such an impression on me when I first met her. It is not her beauty, although her beauty is considerable. It is that she emanates an almost mystical quality of solitude: not solemnity, for she is always animated, either laughing or driving a point home with an upraised finger, but a sovereign, inviolate aloneness.

I had prepared a long list of questions, but now, in her presence, I didn't know where to begin. The unexpectedly complicated business of entering her house had unsettled me: the taxi-driver who dropped me at a distance and sped away; the camera-wielding intelligence agents who loitered by her gate; the smiling policeman who inquired politely after the name of my hotel. After these sinister preliminaries, the normalcy of her house and the calm authority of her presence come almost as a jolt.

I glanced at my notes. Most of my questions were about her party's policies, SLORC's machinations, and so on. I knew now what her answers would be. She meets with foreign reporters almost daily, and her answers are unvarying; they could hardly be otherwise, considering how often the questions are repeated.

She never leaves any doubt about her opposition to foreign investment in Burma under the current regime, although at the time we spoke she stopped short of calling for economic sanctions. Also by implication, she is critical of attempts to lure tourists to Burma. She is unequivocal in her criticism of a so-called 'constitutional convention' that was called by SLORC three years ago: the constitution that was proposed, she points out, would effectively institutionalize military rule, since it reserves a large proportion of seats for military appointees. At the same time, she is generally nonconfrontational in her references to the current regime; she rarely even uses the term SLORC, preferring to use the phrase 'the authorities'.

As I listened to these answers, I knew what I really wanted to ask: I wanted to know what it was like to be under house arrest for six years; what it meant to be separated from one's spouse and one's children; to be offered the option of leaving and turning it down. I thought of my own family, thousands of miles away, and the pain of even a brief separation; of the times I'd found myself looking at my watch and wondering whether my children were asleep or at play.

Her gateside meetings, I'd noticed, were attended by dozens of foreigners. Only a few were reporters and journalists; most were tourists and travellers. They were people like me, members of the world's vast, newspaper-reading middle class, people who took it for granted that there are no heroes among us. But Suu Kyi had proved us wrong. She lived the same kind of life, attended the same classes, read the same books and magazines, got into the same arguments. And she had shown us that the apparently soft and yielding world of books and words could sometimes forge a very fine kind of steel.

I, too, had come on a pilgrimage of sorts. What I really wanted to know was 'Where did you find the courage to do what you have done? What gave you the strength?' And what could one possibly learn of this in an hour — or two hours, or even a hundred? It would take a poet or a novelist years of labour to find a way of understanding what she had done.

The futility of my prepared questions made them inevitable. 'So many people around the world marvel at how you survived those years of house arrest', I said. 'In a way, house arrest must be worse than prison —'

She interrupted me with a laugh. 'Sometimes I thought it would be better in prison', she said, 'because I wouldn't have to cope with keeping the house clean.'

Every time it rained, she said, the roof sprang new leaks, and she had to run up and down the stairs positioning buckets. 'It was a great nuisance. Sometimes I thought, I wonder if it leaks at Insein jail? Whether the prisoners have to run around with buckets to catch the leaks?'

'Did Buddhism help?' I asked.

'Yes', she said. 'Buddhist meditation helped because it created a sense of awareness and a sense of calm.'

'What was it like', I asked, 'the first time you saw your children after those years of house arrest?'

She paused to reflect. 'I didn't see them together', she said. 'My elder son came first, you see. He was fifteen when I last saw him, and he had already taken on his adolescent shape. But my younger son was eleven, and he was still a little boy. When I saw him again, he had changed completely. He had changed physically. If I had seen him out on the street, I would not have known he was my son. I was very happy that nothing had happened — that nothing had really affected the closeness between us.'

She stopped. She evidently found it difficult, possibly distasteful, to talk about her family to a stranger. I felt that I had trespassed, in a small way. Like Suu Kyi, I was brought up to believe in the appropriateness of a strict separation between the public and the private, the political and the domestic. In this view, it is wrong as well as unseemly to reduce a vast political movement to the career of a single leader — to identify the aspirations of millions of people with the life of an individual.

The irony is that nothing better illustrates the passing of these values than Suu Kyi's predicament. In the postmodern world, politics is everywhere a matter of symbols, and the truth is that Suu Kyi is her own greatest political asset. It is only because Burma's 1988 democracy movement had a symbol, personified in Suu Kyi, that the world remembers it and continues to exert pressure on the current regime. Otherwise, the world would almost certainly have forgotten Burma's slain and dispersed democrats just as quickly as it has forgotten many others like them in the past.

The golf-playing generals who run Burma are, of course, well aware of this situation. If it were not for Suu Kyi and the increasingly vocal support for her abroad, SLORC's leaders would have scarcely a worry as they teed off on the links. Under house arrest, Suu Kyi was a living reproach to the regime, and a bar to many foreign investors. By releasing her, the junta achieved a minor propaganda coup.

SLORC is headed by four of the Burmese Army's senior generals. The man who is widely believed to be the brains behind the regime's adroit manoeuvrings over the last several years is Lieutenant General Khin Nyunt, the longtime chief of Burma's intelligence apparatus and a political operator of formidable skill. After the events of 1988, SLORC moved quickly to 'liberalize' the economy and invite foreign investment. No one knows exactly how much money the regime has attracted (the government claims to have got $3 billion), but the single largest investment is a billion-dollar gas pipeline financed by the French company Total and the American energy conglomerate Unocal.

SLORC takes particular pride in what it has done to end the forty-eight-year-old civil war with the country's ethnic insurgents. Again through shrewd political manoeuvring, SLORC has forced many of the country's insurgents to negotiate. Fifteen groups have concluded ceasefire agreements with Rangoon, and the official press frequently claims that these agreements show that the insurgents have entered 'the legal fold'.

When I mentioned the ceasefires, Suu Kyi said, 'There were reports in the Thai papers a couple of weeks ago that there is a constant flow of arms across the border, which indicates that the insurgents are continuing to accumulate arms. That does not sound very much as though they were preparing for permanent peace.' I had already decided that I wanted to investigate the government's claims for myself.

In SLORC's official usage, Burma is now Myanmar, Rangoon is now Yangon, Karenni is now Kayah, and so on. But most of the people I spoke to used the old forms. As I was rising to leave, I asked Suu Kyi to resolve the dilemma; since she is effectively the country's elected leader, she had as good a right as anyone to decide what it should be called.

'I think it's very foolish', she said. 'The excuse [that the authorities] gave was that Burma was a colonial name and referred only to the Burmese people, and Myanmar included all the other ethnic groups. This is just not true. Myanmar is a literary form of *Bama*, which means Burmese. So what it is all about I do not know. Some people say it is *yedea* — a propitiatory rite, something to prevent bad fortune. The authorities believe a lot in astrology.'

'Would you rather I used the old names?' I asked.

She laughed. 'Yes, please use the old forms', she said. 'As support for a sensible way of looking at things. I do not like narrow-mindedness. Even if these names were given by the British colonialists, so what? After all, India is called India, and not Bharat; and China is China. I think if you have enough confidence in yourself you should not worry about what you are called.'

When I stepped out on University Avenue, people had begun to gather around the gates. It was a Saturday afternoon: they were sitting in rows, opposite the gate, waiting for Aung San Suu Kyi to appear. Their presence there once recorded could mean anything from imprisonment and interrogation to lost jobs and forfeited pensions. But still they came, in a slow trickle, walking quickly and self-consciously past the walled mansions and manicured lawns of University Avenue, past the knots of intelligence men and informers who were standing beneath the shade-trees, smoking cheroots and chewing betel. Bearing the pure light of hope in their eyes they came to sit at the gate and wait for Aung San Suu Kyi.

Two days after my meeting with Aung San Suu Kyi I heard that fighting had broken out on the Thai border, between the Burmese army and a small rebel contingent from an ethnic group called the Karenni. There was no mention of this in the Burmese media: they continued to list the Karenni among the groups that had been brought back to the 'legal fold' through SLORC's policy of seeking ceasefires.

Many of my own perplexities about Burma were reflected

in the dissonance between these contradictory reports. I began to ask myself: what is 'Burma' (or 'Myanmar' for that matter)? What does it mean to use a single name, for an entity that has been divided against itself for much of its contemporary history? Why is it that media accounts invariably reproduce this division by concentrating either on the areas under the control of Rangoon, or on the insurgents' territories? Are these two aspects of 'Burma' really so distant from one another as to be unbridgeable by the written word? Or is it the case that here — as in many families — rebellion and violence are aspects of intimacy rather than distance?

On another plane, was it possible that insurgencies could be defeated by force of arms, as SLORC was trying to do? This was, after all, a policy that had been actively espoused by the West in Malaysia and Indonesia in the 1950s and 60s, and had been proved effective at enormous human cost. This was one of the reasons why Burma's junta had succeeded in garnering support amongst its South-east Asian neighbours, many of whom desired stability in the region above all else.

I recalled an anecdote told to me by a Western diplomat in Bangkok: Thailand's immensely respected monarch, King Bhumibol, had once remarked to him that democracy in Burma would have the same effect it had had in Bosnia, only worse. If this was so, what did it mean for the prospects of democracy in multi-ethnic societies?

And further still, who *were* the Karenni insurgents? A glance at a standard reference work told me that Burma's Karenni population is concentrated largely in a small outlying province of eastern Burma; I learnt that they consider themselves to be close kin of the Karen, to the south and that their name, which means 'red Karen' in Burmese is derived from the colour of their national costume. I discovered that the Karenni's 'armed struggle' for independence had begun in 1946 and had continued virtually without interruption ever since.

I found myself marvelling at the sheer longevity of this conflict. What had driven the Karenni to fight so long, with such tenacity and persistence? The territory for which they sought independence had no major urban centres and its population, of some three hundred thousand, was itself divided into ten different ethnic groups. What could nationhood possibly mean for a landlocked, thinly populated tract of forest? What made it worth dying for; for sacrificing three generations?

I began to be very curious about what 'freedom' meant for the Karenni. Did it mean democracy and the rule of law, or merely the right to establish yet another ethnic enclave?

I decided that I would go into their part of Burma to find out.

The fighting between the Burmese army and the Karenni insurgents started on Christmas Eve, 1995, when SLORC launched a surprise assault on a remote checkpoint deep inside the forests and mountains of eastern Burma. The offensive was in its second week when I flew to the border town of Mae Hong Son, in north-western Thailand.

It was a clear day, and I watched in awe as the red, riverine plains of the south changed into jagged, densely forested mountains, a pristine landscape of misted valleys and towering ridges. I could see no sign of any habitation until Mae Hong Son itself appeared suddenly in my window, a string of teakwood buildings nestled in a deep valley.

At first glance, Mae Hong Son seemed to be a quiet

and prosperous frontier town. It was hard to imagine that a war was being fought in the surrounding mountains. I was surprised by the number of hotels on offer. I picked a hotel at random. Within half an hour, my contacts in Mae Hong Son, members of a Burmese student group, sent a guide to take me back across the Burma border into a Karenni-held area that was currently under attack.

We rented a motor scooter and went rattling off down a dirt track that ended at a village near the foot of the mountains. We waded across a stream and started climbing. It was about five in the afternoon, and the sun had already dipped behind a ridge. Following a steeply ascending trail, we stepped from twilight into the darkness of a densely canopied forest. Neither my guide nor I had thought to bring a flashlight; he was wearing rubber sandals and I a pair of thin-soled leather shoes.

I began to regret my precipitate departure. Clawing at the undergrowth to keep from falling, I feared I would end up with a snake in my fist. By the time we stumbled into the students' base camp, hours later, exhaustion had erased every thought from my mind. It was all I could do to stay on my feet.

Half a dozen young guerrillas dressed in camouflage fatigues were squatting around a campfire by a bamboo hut, playing guitars. A heavyset, thickly bearded man detached himself from the group and stepped over to meet me. He introduced himself as the commander of the regiment. He looked me over as I sat panting on a rock. After a moment's hesitation, he asked, a little shyly, 'Are you Indian?' I then noticed that his spoken English sounded oddly like my own. I nodded, and, through a veil of exhaustion, took another look at him. Suddenly, I sat up. 'And you?' I asked.

'My parents were Indian', he said, with a smile. 'But I'm Burmese.'

After my ordeal in the jungle, I was not quite prepared for such an eminently postmodern encounter: my astonishment must have been evident in my face, for the commander began to laugh.

He was called Ko Sonny, but his given name, I learned, was Mahinder Singh. He was in his early thirties and had been 'in the jungle' almost eight years. His family had been settled in Burma for three generations. His parents were born there; his father was Sikh and his mother Hindu, both from families of well-to-do Indian businessmen.

I was disconcerted listening to Sonny in the flickering firelight. I was sure that our relatives had known one another once in Burma: his had chosen to stay and mine hadn't. Except for a few years and a couple of turns of fate, each of us could have been in the other's place.

I spent the night on a bamboo pallet in Sonny's hut. The next day, I was jolted awake before dawn by the sound of a Burmese Army artillery barrage. After groping for a match, I stepped outside to find Sonny talking into a walkie-talkie. The Burmese Army had launched an assault on a Karenni position in an adjoining valley.

The fighting was a good distance away, but the sound of gunfire came rolling up the misted mountainside with uncanny clarity, the rattle of small-arms fire clearly audible in the lulls between exploding artillery shells. The noise sent flocks of parakeets shooting out of the mountainside's tangled canopy.

With daybreak, I had my first look at the camp — a string of thatched bamboo huts arranged along a mountain stream. A great deal of thought had gone into the camp's planning. The plumbing was far from rudimentary: water was piped directly into bathrooms and showers from a stream. There was a dammed pond teeming with fish and, near by, a pen full of pigs.

Next to each hut was a vegetable patch. Once Sonny had ascertained that the fighting was not headed our way, he picked up a watering can and waded into a patch of bok choy. Following his lead, the others put aside their battle gear and disappeared into their pumpkin trellises and mustard beds, like a troop of Sunday gardeners.

'Growing food is as important to our survival as fighting', Ko Sonny explained apologetically. 'We do this before we go on patrol.'

We set out an hour or so later, a detachment of half a dozen student fighters, with Sonny in the lead. Once we had crossed the border, an unmarked forest trail, Sonny and his men reclaimed a cache of ageing M-16s and slung them over their shoulders.

We climbed on to a ridge, where I found myself gazing at a majestic spectacle of forested gorges, mountain peaks, and a sky of crisp, pellucid blue. The shelling was sporadic now: occasionally the forest canopy would silently sprout a mushroom cloud of smoke, the accompanying blast climbing leisurely up the slope moments later.

Mae Hong Son was clearly visible, a smudge in the floor of a tip-tilted valley. While Sonny counted off the calibre of the exploding shells — 120 mm., 81 mm. — I turned his binoculars on the town and spotted my hotel.

Sonny pointed to the Karenni post we were to visit.

It was called Naung Lon and it was built around a peak that reared high above the surrounding spurs and ridges. From a distance the camp looked more like a stockade than a guerilla outpost. We entered through a hidden gate in an outer wall of sharpened bamboo stakes. Then we crossed, in succession, a moat of sharply-angled trenches, a barbed-wire barrier and a twenty-foot clearing that led uphill to a circle of heavily sandbagged gun emplacements. The fighters' living quarters were dug deep into the red earth of the mountain's flattened tip, a warren of roofed bunkers, protected by earthworks and timber struts.

We were met by a Karenni colonel: a tall stooped man, with melancholy eyes and an air of slightly regretful doggedness. He showed me around the camp, pointing proudly to a volleyball court and a sunken hall that served as both mess and prayer-room. Cooks were busy in the field-kitchen, carrying enamel plates of rice and fish-paste to soldiers at their posts, flinging leftovers at a brood of circling chickens. Two freshly-bathed teen-age fighters sat playing a quiet game of chess, on a tree-stump, with their M-16s across their knees. In a nearby bunker, off-duty soldiers were strumming guitars and singing what sounded like a hymn.

The colonel and his men were all devout Christians. The colonel himself happened to be a Baptist, his ancestors having been converted by American missionaries in the late nineteenth century, but there were also several Catholics among his men. The timing of the first Burmese attack still rankled with the colonel. 'Even the world wars stopped for Christmas,' he said, 'but nothing stops the Burmese army.'

The colonel's eyes flickered constantly over the thickly forested mountains around us as we spoke. The colonel pointed in the direction of the mountain where the fighting was taking place: it was about four miles to the south, screened from us by a delicate tracery of overlapping spurs and ridges. It was known locally as Rambo Hill.

A Burmese encampment was visible from where we stood, a ridge and a valley away, swathed in a thin, early morning haze. Through the colonel's binoculars I could see wisps of smoke curling out of the earthworks around the post: like the Karenni, the Burmese soldiers were eating their morning meal.

The colonel knew that camp well. The Karenni had held it until just three months ago. Until quite recently the Karenni controlled a broad swathe of mineral- and timber-rich territory, extending all the way from the Thai border to the west bank of the Salween river, some fifty miles into Burma. Now they were reduced to a thin, rapidly fraying ribbon along the border.

The colonel's arm described a semi-circle as he pointed to the Burmese positions on the mountaintops around us. To the north, guarded by a range of blue, towering peaks lay the Golden Triangle, and what was once the fiefdom of Khun Sa, a notorious drug-lord who had recently made peace with SLORC. Khun Sa's 'surrender' meant that the peaks overlooking Karenni territory would pass into SLORC's control while freeing a large number of troops for redeployment. Sixteen Burmese battalions were already concentrated in this sector, four more were said to be on their way. Soon the Karenni army would be facing a force of about ten thousand men. Against this they could muster a total strength of about six hundred, with an additional two hundred irregulars. The colonel knew he was defending a hopeless position, and had already made plans to evacuate.

Later, on the way back to the student camp, I remarked to Sonny that I didn't see how the Karenni army could possibly escape defeat.

Sonny laughed. The Karenni, he pointed out, had been fighting against dire odds for fifty years. Many regarded the war against SLORC as a direct continuation of the war against the Japanese. Some Karenni families had been at war for three generations, and many of their fighters had spent their entire lives in refugee camps.

What does it take, I found myself wondering, to sustain an insurgency for fifty years, to go on fighting a war that the rest of the world has almost forgotten?

The next day, I returned to Mae Hong Son and went to see Mr Abel Tweed, the Foreign Minister of the Karenni National Progressive Party, in his small back-alley office. A voluble square-jawed man, Mr Tweed delved into a makeshift archive housed in a cupboard. 'We have always been independent,' he announced, 'and we have the documents to prove it.'

Leafing through the papers he handed me, I saw that he was right: the British had clearly recognized Karenni autonomy in the late nineteenth century and had rejected the option of annexing the Karenni territories to Burma proper. Their reasons were not altruistic. 'It is evident that the country is perfectly worthless in itself', one British administrator wrote of the Karenni area. 'It is almost impracticable, for even an elephant.'

It was the Second World War that thrust the Karenni's 'impracticable' country centre stage. Looking for Asian partners in the struggle against the Japanese, the Allied powers encouraged several ethnic groups along the borders of Burma to rise against the occupying army. The Karenni, the Karen, and the Kachin eagerly embraced the Allies. A number of British and American military personnel took up residence in their villages, and some of them virtually assumed the role of tribal elders.

The Karenni, along with the Karen and the Kachin, were spectacularly effective guerrillas, and their loyalty proved to be important to the Allies. The repayment that these groups expected was independence. To this day, they nurture a bitter historical grievance that the debt was never paid.

Abel Tweed was born long after the war, but his voice shook as he talked of the British departure from Burma. 'The British knew that the Karenni were not a part of Burma', he said. 'But the Karenni are a small people; they forgot us.'

There are six thousand or so displaced Karenni refugees, and they are divided among five camps. Until fairly recently, these camps were in Burma, on a narrow tract of land controlled by the insurgents, but the steady advance of Burmese troops has gradually pushed the camps back over the border into Thailand. The camps are now clustered around Mae Hong Son — a tourist town which promotes an activity known as 'hill-tribe trekking'. The camps have come to be linked to this tourist entertainment through an odd symbiosis. The women of one Karenni subgroup have traditionally worn heavy brass rings to elongate their necks, and these women are now ticketed tourist attractions, billed as 'giraffe women': their refugee camps are a feature of the hill-tribe-trekking routes. In effect, tourism has transformed these camps, with their tragic histories of oppression, displacement, and misery, into counterfeits of timeless rural simplicity — waxwork versions of the very past that their inhabitants have irretrievably lost. Karenni fighters returning from their battles on the front lines become, as it were, mirrors in which their visitors can discover an imagined Asian innocence.

I had a heightened sense of what it means to live with a half-century-old insurgency when I set out to visit the Karenni's refugee camp No. 5, to the south of Mae Hong Son. The camp is deep in the forest, on the banks of the Pai, a fast-flowing mountain river. The only access road is a dirt track that winds steeply through the mountains before descending to the bottom of a gorge where the distinction between road and river becomes purely notional. To get to the camp I had to ford the Pai eleven times on my rented motorcycle. I considered myself lucky to have escaped with no more serious injury than a severe exhaust burn.

The camp appears suddenly, around a bend in the river, a cluster of bamboo-walled dwellings grouped around a high-school, a clinic and an open-sided Baptist church. With its rope-bridge and its wisps of woodsmoke the settlement blends so perfectly into its setting of towering mist-shrouded forests that it could easily be mistaken for a long-settled mountain village. In fact it was built in 1992, when the Karenni were forced to relocate from an earlier, more convenient site. For the Karenni the war has meant, most of all, an enforced adaptation to nomadism.

There are five major Karenni refugee camps and together they form a minuscule, tight-knit nation-on-the-move, consisting of some six thousand people. Men of military age circulate between front-line outposts, while the political leadership shuttles constantly between the five camps.

Camp number five's high school gives it a special place in the archipelago of Karenni encampments: it draws teenage children from all the other camps. Every evening the camp's lanes are filled with the murmurs of high-school students reciting their lessons — not, as it happens, in their own language but in Burmese. The camps have been located inside Thailand for several years: a country that is one of the great success stories of the contemporary world, with an excellent educational system. Yet very few Karenni are literate in Thai and their curricula are still closely modeled on those of Burma's state-run schools. A curious paradox of this long-lived insurgency is that culturally the Karenni continue to look towards Rangoon. The freewheeling ways of contemporary Thailand inspires unease in many Karenni. 'I never go into their cities', the Deputy Minister of Education told me, gesturing in the direction of Mae Hong Son. 'It is hard for us to live among them, even though we are grateful for what they have done for us.'

In a large house at one end of camp number five, after days of futile pursuit, I finally managed to catch up with the highest-ranking Karenni leader, the Prime Minister, Mr Aung Than Lay. He proved to be a mild-mannered man with a benign, grandfatherly smile. Speaking through a translator he explained that he was one of the last remaining veterans from the earliest days of the Karenni struggle. 'When I started to fight I was a boy and I knew nothing', he said. He had enlisted in a British infantry unit in 1946. Two years later, when fighting broke out in Karenni State he deserted to join the rebels. He has been fighting ever since.

We talked at length about Burmese politics and Karenni history. He insisted repeatedly that his group would not compromise on its demand for an independent Karenni state: 'According to our policy, we the Karenni are an independent country. We have always been independent, we have never been under the Burmese and we have never been a part of Burma. That is why we are fighting, because we were free all along. We are fighting a war of resistance against an invader.'

'The Bible says the unrighteous shall perish', the Prime Minister's translator added. 'We will continue despite everything because we are fighting the good fight.'

Although I was sympathetic to this argument, I had doubts about what 'independence' might mean for a tiny, landlocked state that would inevitably have to depend on its neighbours for its economic survival. But in talking to Karenni leaders, my objections began to seem curiously academic and irrelevant. The fact was that they had practical experience of what it takes to sustain a population: their tiny, putative nation would not have survived for decades if they had not succeeded in improvising an economy of their own.

The working of this twilight economy was explained to me at a Karenni refugee camp, by a group of senior officials, including the KNPP's current second-in-command, a thoughtful, bespectacled ex-history teacher called Raymond Htoo. For the last several years, Mr Htoo said, the group's principal source of income was timber, from the territory under its control. The Karenni granted logging concessions to Thai businessmen, in exchange for a fifth of the profits. In addition they also levied taxes on the timber at their border checkpoints. The combined revenues amounted to millions of dollars. The Thai timbermen were notably efficient in denuding the Karenni territories of their primary forests: in 1995, said Mr Htoo, some fifteen thousand tons of timber, valued at $1,000 a ton, had passed through the Karenni checkpoints.

It was these profits that lay behind the current escalation in the conflict. According to Mr Htoo, Burmese army commanders had recently negotiated their own deals with Thai timber companies: hence their determination to seize control of the KNPP's territory.

Their other objective, Mr Htoo said, was to end the cross-border black-market trade. In the past the KNPP had earned considerable sums by imposing tariffs on the goods that flowed across its checkpoints: cattle heading towards Thai abattoirs, from all over Burma and as far away as eastern India; heading in the other direction were electronic appliances and South-east Asian manufactured goods. The one kind of trade they never permitted, the KNPP officials insisted, was drug-trafficking because it violated their devoutly Christian beliefs.

The Burmese army's current objective was to strangle the KNPP economically, the officials said. But in their view this was a doomed strategy: their network of supporters and sympathizers was strong enough, even inside Burma, to raise substantial sums locally — 'for protection' — from merchants, timber companies and traders in their state. And as for the cross-border trade it had merely shifted location: it was now being conducted on boats, moored on the Salween river, fifty miles across the border.

'Unless there is a major transformation inside Burma', Mr Htoo said, 'this trade cannot be blocked. The Burmese cannot hope to stop this trade by force. The border is unsealable. Even if they take all the border posts and all our territory it won't matter. They cannot build a Great Wall of China.'

'What would happen', I asked, 'if SLORC and its allies were to put diplomatic pressure on the Thai authorities to evict you? How would your organization survive without the camps?'

Mr Htoo had an answer ready. 'That cannot happen', he said. 'Most of the people in the camps are non-combatants. They are protected by international law. Those of us who are fighters would pick up our weapons and go into the mountains. It is our land: SLORC would not be able to find us. They can overrun our strong points but our strategy is mobile. The fortified posts are just a trap. They cannot hold them long. We can inflict heavy casualties on them with little risk to our men.'

An insurgency, I was beginning to realize, is not just an army and a gathering of camp-followers. It is simultaneously a cause, an archive, an economy: an institution which provides for itself and develops a life that it will not cheaply relinquish.

'What about the future?' I asked. 'If Aung San Suu Kyi and the National League for Democracy came to power would you be willing to end the war and join a federal union of Burma?'

Like other Karenni officials I had spoken to, Mr Htoo was guarded in his answer. 'Whether we join Aung San Suu Kyi or not depends on the future constitution', he said. 'If the NLD draws up a constitution that is a social contract, ensuring a place for the Karenni people, then that is acceptable. But each state must have sovereignty and the right to self-determination.'

I told them that when I met her in Rangoon, Aung San Suu Kyi had emphasized her keenness to reach an agreement with Burma's ethnic minorities and had acknowledged their concerns.

Mr Htoo nodded doubtfully. 'With Aung San Suu Kyi maybe peace can come back to Burma', he said. 'If she is not assassinated. Aung San was good to the minorities so the Burmans killed him. With Aung San Suu Kyi it may be the same. Some Burmese politicians want to maintain "Greater Burma" at all costs.'

I often wished that there were some way of determining the opinion of the refugee rank-and-file. Like the other ethnic organizations along the Burma border, the KNPP is run on authoritarian lines: there are no elections for its leadership posts and it is impossible to know how representative the leadership's views are.

Wandering around the Karenni camps I began to suspect that the refugees had already had enough of their 'independence'. I noticed that portraits of Aung San Suu Kyi hung in almost every dwelling. I suspect that in a free election the Karenni, like most Burmese, would vote overwhelmingly for Aung San Suu Kyi.

In another matter Mr Htoo was soon vindicated. Within days, Karenni fighters ambushed a SLORC supply convoy on its way to the newly-captured post on Rambo Hill, inflicting heavy casualties on the Burmese with very little loss to themselves.

In April there was news that the Burmese army had overrun the last remaining strips of territory under Karenni control. But I suspect the Burmese army is still no closer to victory than the Karenni are to defeat: neither term has any meaning in a circumstance of institutionalized war.

I had come to the border hoping to find that democracy would provide a solution to Burma's unresolved civil war. By the time I left, I was no longer sure what the solution could be.

'The majority of Burmans think that democracy is the only problem', a member of the powerful Kachin minority reminded me. 'But ethnic groups took up arms when Rangoon had a democratic government. A change to democracy won't help. The outside world expects too much from Suu Kyi. From our point of view, we don't care who governs — the weaker the better.'

There are thousands of putative nationalities in the world today; at least sixteen of them are situated on Burma's borders. It is hard to imagine that the inhabitants of these areas would be well served by becoming separate states. A hypothetical Karenni state, for example, would be landlocked, with the population of a medium-sized town: it would not be less dependent on its larger neighbours simply because it had a flag and a seat at the U.N.

Burma's borders are undeniably arbitrary, the product of a capricious colonial history. But colonial officials cannot reasonably be blamed for the arbitrariness of the lines they drew. All boundaries are artificial: there is no such thing as a 'natural' nation, which has journeyed through history with its boundaries and ethnic composition intact. In a region as heterogeneous as South-east Asia, any boundary is sure to be arbitrary. On balance, Burma's best hopes for peace lie in maintaining intact the larger and more inclusive entity that history, albeit absent-mindedly, bequeathed to its population almost half a century ago.

Aung San Suu Kyi is the one figure in Burma who has popular support, both among ethnic Burmans and among many minorities, to start a process of national reconciliation. But even Suu Kyi would find it difficult to alter the historical borders. In the event of a total military withdrawal, it is possible that some insurgent groups would attempt to reclaim the territories they once controlled. A rekindling of the insurgencies would almost certainly lead to a rapid erosion of Suu Kyi's popular support. Suu Kyi is aware that she cannot govern effectively without the support of the Army, and she had been at pains to build bridges with middle-ranking officers as well as with the rank-and-file, repeatedly stressing her heritage as the daughter of the Army's founder.

Somewhere in the unruffled reaches of her serenity, Suu Kyi has probably prepared herself for the ordeal that lies ahead: the possibility that she, an apostle of non-violence, may yet find herself constrained to wage war.

There is no mystery about why Burma's rebels never lack for recruits.

On the border I met a deserter from the Burmese army who had recently joined the student regiment. This was the story he told me: his name was Zin Myin Thein and he was twenty years old. He was an ethnic Burman from the area of Prome, in central Burma and his father was a landless farm labourer. In 1994 the local SLORC military commander had ordered the area's civilian officials to send in a certain number of conscripts. A lottery was held, with an entry for each household in the area. The households that were selected were given the option of sending either a male recruit or a cash contribution of 3,000 Kyat, about five years income for a civil servant (a concession was made for widows).

The luck of the draw had sent the eighteen-year-old Zin Myin Thein into the army in the summer of 1994. After four months training he was sent to join a regiment that was guarding a large hydro-electric project in the Karenni area. Upon arrival he discovered that his tasks were principally agricultural and janitorial. Like most Burmese army units in outlying areas, his regiment sustained itself partly by foraging in the countryside and partly by growing its own food. The recruits' duties consisted of working long hours in the fields, and as servants in the officers' households.

According to Zin Myin Thein, he and a few other recruits made plans to desert on 16 September 1995, but their escape was thwarted by a Karenni attack on the power-station. Eventually he deserted alone, on the 17th, while on guard duty, with his standard-issue G-3 assault rifle.

This story would seem incredible were it not for the fact that several similar accounts have been reported to human rights activists.

In Rangoon, I heard the story from the other side, told by a recently retired military officer who had been posted in the frontier areas through much of his career. Lacking reliable supplies from headquarters, he like many of his fellow officers, had been pushed to find other ways of providing for his troops. In desperation, he said, some officers would simply seize local resources, like mines and fisheries and auction them off to the highest bidder. Or else they would requisition provisions and labour from local villages. As a professional soldier he had felt keenly the humiliation of being reduced to this form of banditry.

I spent a lot of time with Sonny. He was very good company: always witty, ready to laugh, enormously intelligent, and so devoid of macho posturing that it was easy to forget he was a hardened combatant. When we were in the mountains, he would go striding along at the head of a column, looking every inch the guerrilla, with his dangling cheroot and his cradled M-16. When he came down to visit Mae Hong Son, he would exchange his fatigues for jeans and a T-shirt, and it was hard to tell him apart from a holidaying business executive.

I asked him once, 'As someone of Indian descent, do you ever feel out of place as the commander of a regiment of Burmese students?'

'You don't understand', he said. 'I don't think of myself as Indian. I hated being Indian. As a child, everywhere I went people would point to me and say *kala* ("foreigner"), although I had never left Burma in my whole life. I hated that word. I wanted to show them: that is not what I am; I am not a *kala*. This is why I am here now.'

Sonny had grown up in a tiny provincial town, Loikaw, the capital of Burma's erstwhile Karenni province. While he was attending the university in Rangoon (he studied physics there for four years), Sonny championed the cause of Karenni and other minority students. With the start of the democracy movement, in 1988, he returned home and helped to organize peaceful demonstrations in Loikaw. He was arrested on 18 September and released ten days later. Fearing rearrest, he immediately planned his escape to the border.

On the night of 6 October, Sonny left Loikaw with a group of activists. They made their way to a rebel base, where Karenni insurgents gave them a warm welcome and provided them with land and supplies so that they could set up bases of their own. Sonny and his fellow-activists had never held a gun.

After eight years of fighting, Sonny has no illusions about the 'armed struggle'. 'We're fighting because there is no other way to get SLORC to talk', he told me. 'For us, armed struggle is just a strategy. We are not militants here: we can see how bad war is.'

I asked, 'Have you ever thought of trying other political strategies?'

'Of course', he said. 'Do you think I like to get up in the morning and think of killing? Killing someone from my own country, who is forced to fight by dictators? I would like to try other things — politics, lobbying. But the students chose me to command this regiment. I can't just leave them.'

Sonny has paid a price for his decision to leave Loikaw. His girlfriend, a Burmese in Rangoon, gave up waiting for him, and married someone else. In 1994, his mother died of a heart attack; Sonny found out months afterward from a passing trader. She was, he said, the person he was closest to.

The student dissidents are now in their late twenties or early thirties. They had once aspired to become technicians and engineers, doctors and pharmacists. Those hopes are gone. They have no income to speak of, and their contacts with Thai society are few.

The truth is that they now have very limited options. Legally, they are not allowed either to work or to study in Thailand; to seek asylum abroad as refugees, they would have to enter a holding camp in southern Thailand while their papers were processed. Those whose applications were rejected would risk being deported to Burma, and once there they would almost certainly be imprisoned, or worse. The alternative is to join the underworld of illegal foreign workers in Thailand, vanishing into a nightmarish half-life of crime, drugs, and prostitution. They have been pushed into a situation where the jungle is the sanest choice available.

For the insurgents, Aung San Suu Kyi offers the only remaining hope of returning to their country with dignity and reclaiming their lives. When Sonny heard that I had met Aung San Suu Kyi in Rangoon, he wanted to know exactly what she had said. I played him some of my tape, including a segment in which she answered a question about her commitment to nonviolence.

'I do not think violence will really get us what we want', he said. 'Some of the younger people disagree. In 1988, a lot of them went across the border because they said the only way you can topple this government is by force of arms. And not just the younger people. Even very mature, seasoned people have said to me, "You can't do it without arms. This government is the type that understands only violence". But my argument is: All right, supposing that all those who wanted democracy decided that the only way was through force of arms and we all took up arms. Would we not be setting a precedent for more violence in the future? Would we not be endorsing the view that those who have the superior might of arms are those who will rule the country? That is something that I cannot support. But we have always said that we will never, never disown those who have decided to take up arms, because we understand how they feel. I tried to dissuade some of the young people who fled across the border, but who am I to force them to stay? If I could guarantee their liberty and their safety, if I could say to them, "You will not be arrested, you will not be tortured", I would. But, since I could not, I did not even think I had the moral right to stop them leaving.'

When the tape was finished, I asked Sonny what he would do if he was pushed out of Thailand as well. 'What if the Thais decide to cut off your supplies or starve you out of Thailand?'

'It wouldn't be easy to starve us out', Sonny said. 'We've been here a long time; we now have many connections with the people of this region; some Burmese students have married Thai villagers. We can survive in the jungle: we are used to it now. That is why our camps are self-sufficient. We could disappear into the jungle for a long time; we are not unprepared.'

If it came to the worst, Sonny was saying that he and his men would disappear into the jungle to carry on their war from behind the lines. And it made sense: the poppy fields of the Golden Triangle, with their warring drug lords, were just a short walk away. Someone as resourceful as Sonny could disappear there indefinitely if he were pushed: the jungle was all too ready to claim him.

It was cold in the camp that night, with a bitter wind blowing through the slatted bamboo walls. I spent much of the night awake, trying to think of what it meant to live in a circumstance in which the jungle seemed to be the best of all available options.

I awoke next morning to find a pile of books by my head. Sonny had wrapped a few books in a towel as a makeshift pillow, and the bundle had come undone at night. The books were language primers, workbooks, and the like, except for one: a hardbound 1991 edition entitled 'The Transformation of War'. The author, Martin van Creveld, I discovered later, is something of an oracle among doomsday theorists.

I flipped the book open, and I became riveted. I began to make notes in my diary. 'Van Creveld is arguing that the state's historic monopoly of violence ended with the

"Thirty Years War of 1914–45"; that nuclear weapons have rendered war, as waged by states, nearly obsolete, because inconceivable; that the world will now be dominated by low-intensity conflict; that states in the conventional sense will give way to bands of warlords; that the distinction between government, army and the people will begin to fall apart as never before, especially in the Third World; that groups such as private mercenary bands, commanded by warlords and even commercial agencies (like the old East India Company), will once again take over the function of war-making; that "existing distinctions between war and crime will break down".'

Outside the hut, Sonny and his men were busy in the crisp sunlight, tending their patches of cauliflower and mustard. Until then, I had looked upon Sonny as an anachronistic remnant of a dwindling series of 'dirty little Asian wars'. I now saw that I was very likely wrong: what Sonny represented was not the past but a possible future.

I returned to Burma during the last week of July 1996. In the past couple of months, there had been a number of disquieting developments. I wanted to see for myself what the consequences were — for both Aung San Suu Kyi and the country.

Last May, a conference called by Suu Kyi to mark the anniversary of her party's victory in the 1990 election was disrupted when the government arrested more than two hundred and thirty party delegates who planned to attend; many were arrested at their homes or on their way to Rangoon.

Suu Kyi, unable to convene all the delegates, held the conference anyway, as scheduled, between 26 May and 28 May. Thousands gathered outside her gates, one of the largest crowds since her house arrest ended last year. On the last day, she announced that her party would draft a new constitution — a democratic alternative to the one that was being slowly deliberated by the government. Like the party conference itself, the call for a new constitution was a provocative gesture, and for Aung San Suu Kyi an unusually confrontational one. For the first time since her release, Suu Kyi had wrested the initiative away from the government, pushing it on to the defensive. Her party was reinvigorated.

Two weeks later, the government responded. It issued a decree that effectively banned Suu Kyi's gateside meetings: all speeches and any statements that were seen to undermine 'the stability of the State' were prohibited. In case there was any doubt about its objective, the law also prohibited the drafting of a new constitution without the authorization of the state. The decree was issued on 7 June, but it was not immediately put into effect. The government appears to have been unprepared for the vehemence of the international criticism that its actions provoked.

The criticism had been mounting since April, when, as part of an effort to harass and intimidate Suu Kyi's supporters, the authorities had arrested one of her close family friends, Leo Nichols, for operating an unauthorized fax machine. Nichols, an Anglo-Burmese businessman who had served as honorary consul for the Scandinavian countries, was sentenced to three years in prison on 17 May. Five weeks later, he died while in police custody, and the government's account of his death was unsatisfactory. Protests widened. Denmark called for economic sanctions, and asked the European Union to impose them; in the United States, a similar motion was debated in Congress.

The government's reaction was seen at the time to be oddly contradictory. There was even the suggestion that it might be ready to compromise. The likelihood is that the generals were largely indifferent to the international outcry; their concern was that the outcry might influence the leaders attending the July meeting of the Association of South-east Asian Nations (ASEAN), in Jakarta. Burma was still not a member of the association — a legacy of its years of isolation — and membership was essential to establishing the country as a full trading partner in the region. Burma was seeking observer status, the first step in gaining membership. The talk among the Asian nations was now of 'constructive engagement' — the soft diplomacy that only successful trade makes possible. On 20 July, Burma got the recognition it sought. The regime, it seems, was set on buying its own legitimacy.

I arrived in Rangoon on Sunday, 28 July 1996, just in time to make it to the gateside meeting on University Avenue. The week before, the American Secretary of State, Warren Christopher, had been in Jakarta and had censured the government of Burma, but his censure was largely rhetorical and ineffective. He stopped short of sanctions, and I wondered what Suu Kyi's response would be. In the past, she had characteristically hesitated to call for any kind of economic boycott; she had now changed her position. The new wave of foreign investment, she had concluded, merely 'put more money in the pockets of the privileged élite. Sanctions', she said, 'would not hurt the ordinary people of Burma.'

The meeting was a large one — about six thousand people. Looking around, I spotted the familiar faces of several people, some of them occupying the same spots as before, like restaurant regulars. Suu Kyi was, as before at the Sunday meetings, flanked by two senior colleagues from the National League for Democracy.

On my previous visit, I had been astonished by her

performance. She was full of merriment, giggling and flirtatious. Several months later, she was still animated, but the lightheartedness was no longer there.

She had changed. So, too, had the city. The next day, I went downtown, into the main business district, and found that an entire block had been transformed. The graceful but shabby old colonial arcades — untouched, like so much of Rangoon, for decades — had been torn down, and, in a matter of months, had been replaced with a maze of office buildings, hotels, and shops. In a nearby marketplace, I discovered that the value of the currency had dropped by a third, and that the price of foodstuffs had risen dramatically.

I was taken to one of Rangoon's new coffee bars by Ma Thanegi, a friend from my last visit. Ma Thanegi is an artist. She joined the democracy movement in 1988 and became an extremely active member: she even worked as an assistant to Aung San Suu Kyi and was a close friend. But then Ma Thanegi was arrested and was imprisoned for three years. By the time of her release, she had had enough of politics — she wanted to look after her own interests — and she opened an art gallery with an American expatriate.

Ma Thanegi was concerned about recent developments, especially Western trade sanctions. Ma Thanegi's view was that a trade boycott would work only if it were a total boycott, involving all countries. And was that realistic? If only Western companies pulled out, there would be many Asian ones prepared to take their place. These new companies, Ma Thanegi said, would have less regard for Burmese workers and the local environment than those they had replaced.

Ma Thanegi had lived her whole life in Rangoon. She came of age during General Ne Win's Burmese Way to Socialism.

'We lived under self-imposed isolation for decades', she said. 'There was absolutely nothing, no opportunities at all, but we struggled on. Ma Ma', as she refers to Suu Kyi, 'says we have to tighten our belts and think about politics. But there are no more notches to tighten on our belts.'

I saw Aung San Suu Kyi the next day. As I walked through the familiar blue gates, I noticed a striking new addition: a large bamboo-and-thatch pavilion. It had been built to house the delegates of the party conference; most of those who had originally been invited did not get to see it.

When Aung San Suu Kyi appeared, I congratulated her on the success of the conference. With a self-deprecating smile, she described it as 'routine party work'. The achievement, she said, was in SLORC's reaction: it showed 'how nervous SLORC was of the democracy movement'.

Suu Kyi's face seemed strained and tired. It was now more than a year since she'd been freed from house arrest, and I found myself wondering whether her freedom was not in its way as much a burden as a release. It seemed as though the impossibly difficult task of conducting a political life under the conditions imposed on her by SLORC had proved just as hard as the enforced solitude of the preceding years. Those conditions seemed to be making her into a different kind of political figure.

She was quick to confirm the change. After she was released, she said, she made a point of being conciliatory, 'but SLORC did not respond. And we have to carry on with our work. We are not going to sit and wait for SLORC to decide what we want to do. . . . That's not the way politics works.'

Suu Kyi had not, as far I knew, responded publicly to the recent ASEAN meeting, in which Burma was granted its new observer status, and I was eager to know what her thoughts might be. I asked her if she was surprised by the warmth of Burma's welcome.

Suu Kyi dismissed my question. It was only normal that the association should welcome a new member.

Her reply surprised me.

No, she said, really. There was nothing unusual about it.

I persisted. At a time when many nations were talking about taking actions against Burma, the South-east Asian leaders spoke about a policy of constructive engagement, which seemed like an endorsement of the regime.

Again, I was dismissed. Picking her words carefully, she said, 'I don't quite understand why one talks about constructive engagement as being such a problem. Each government has its own policy, and we accept that this is the policy of the ASEAN nations. I sometimes think that this problem is made out to be much bigger than it really is. . . . Just because [these governments] have decided on a policy of constructive engagement, there is no need for us to think of them as our enemies. I do not think it's a case of us and them.'

I was witnessing, I realized, Suu Kyi the tactician. She was choosing her words with such care because she wanted to insure that she did not alienate the leaders of nations who might otherwise think of her as a threat.

I was struck by the differences in Suu Kyi's manner. That other time, I had had several glimpses of her earlier selves — the writer and researcher, the scholar trying to reach for the right words to articulate subtle gradations of truth. She now seemed much more the politician, opaque and often abrupt in her answers. The change was inevitable, perhaps, and possibly necessary, but I still found myself mourning it.

Suu Kyi now had a party line. 'We think', she said, 'that

sanctions are the right thing. Further investment in Burma is not helping the people.' It is, she said, serving only a privileged élite. 'It is increasingly obvious that investments made now in Burma only help to make SLORC richer and richer. And that is an obstacle to democratization.'

I mentioned some of the arguments I had heard — that sanctions will lead only to the Western companies being replaced by their Asian counterparts — and this remark, too, was peremptorily dismissed. Without Western investment, she said, 'I think you will find that the confidence in the Burmese economy will diminish. It is not going to encourage the Asians to come rushing in. On the contrary.'

At my previous meeting with Suu Kyi, I'd asked her whether she was contemplating a call for mass civil disobedience. She had remarked that she couldn't tell me even if she had been, but she'd gone on to add, on a note of barely disguised frustration, that if the people wanted democracy, then they were going to have to do something to get it. When I asked her about civil disobedience this time, my question was curtly dismissed. 'We never discuss our plans in advance', she said. 'You know that.'

Even so, I was left wondering. That morning, I had talked to a diplomat who was certain that if Suu Kyi called for civil disobedience the country would follow. It would grind to a complete standstill, he said. I asked myself if that might be the future.

I left Rangoon the next day, feeling discouraged. The plane was full to capacity, its seats occupied by trim men in suits. They all looked as if they had flown in from the great boom centres of Asia. They were in town to do a deal. I looked down on the receding city, and I thought of a comment that Suu Kyi had made at the end of our meeting. 'I've always told you', she said, 'that we will win . . . that we will establish a democracy in Burma, and I stand by that. But as to when, I cannot predict. I've always said that to you.'

Once the plane had sliced through the dark blanket of Rangoon's monsoon sky, the cabin filled with the whine of laptops logging on — that familiar buzzing sound, not unlike that of mosquitoes, feasting in mid-flight.